BHAGAVAD GITA SIMPLIFIED

&

ARTICLES EXPLORING SRI KRISHNA

Written By

Jayanthinathan

Title : Bhagavad Gita Simplified & Articles Exploring Sri Krishna
Author : Jayanthinathan
Edition : 1st (February, 2024)
ISBN : 9788196942502

Published by

A Venture by -
PRACHI DIGITAL PUBLICATION

Regd. Add.: 254, Khuriyakhatta No. 10, Bindukhatta,
Lalkuan, Nainital - 262402, Uttarakhand, India
Website : www.taneeshapublishers.in
E-mail : taneeshapublishers@gmail.com
Phone : +91 845481 2712, +91 976041 7980

Printed by :
Manipal Technologies Limited, Bengaluru - 560001, Karnataka

Bhagavad Gita Book Dedicated to Three Great Souls

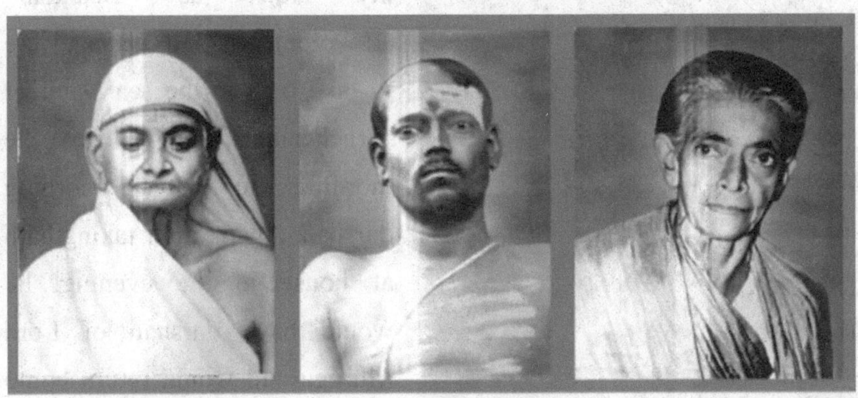

RUKMANI AMMAL (Grand Mother) **SUBRAMANYA IYER** (Father) **KANTHIMATHI AMMAL** (Mother)

Three Great Souls – My Grand Mother Rukmani Ammal, My Father Subramanya Iyer and My Mother Kanthimathi Ammal were responsible for us to lead simple, religious and God-loving life.

Karma Yogis Mother and Grand Mother and Bhakthi Yogi Father had strived their level best to give us a fairly reasonable comfortable living. My mother with support of my grandmother had toiled on daily basis to run a mess and were our breadwinners. Hence both deserved title of Karma Yogis and their poojas, temples and rituals were all confined to kitchen. My Mother's cracked bloody reddish swollen rough palms and her fingers were testimony to her Karma Yogi Title.

My father had devoted completely to Tiruchendur Lord Muruga and all would address my father as "Bhakthar" (Devotee). His daily rituals were to take bath in the sea water of Tiruchendur Temple in the morning to have morning darshan. Again, after taking bath at house in the evening, he would have darshan of Lord Muruga and would return home late in the night only after the temple was closed for the day. His contribution in running the mess was mostly restricted to fetching drinking water to the kitchen. He also supplied drinking water to other householders /schools/ government offices for small fees thereby to keep himself busy. For supplying drinking water, water drum mounted bullock cart was used by my father.

A very small Pillaiyar Idol (photo on left) was installed in a small wooden mandapam in my house. The idol is our house deity and daily pooja was performed by my great grand father and then by my father. One day, my father had asked me to do pooja for the idol. The idol was ceremoniously handed over to me. This is a pride and precious possession presented by my father to me.

Daily till date, I am performing pooja for the same Pillaiyar Idol. Sometimes my wife also would perform pooja to the Pillaiyar. Our Pillaiyar was seen drinking milk (This refers to the worldwide phenomena of Pillaiyar Drinking Milk Episode) provided by my wife and this occurrence was witnessed by self, my daughter and my son apart from the neighbours living in our apartment. Our Pillaiyar was special for us and we are blessed by His Grace. We believe that our Pillaiyar protects us and blesses us 24/7 – 365 days. Our Pillaiyar's Blessings are sought for release of this book - Bhagavad Gita Simplified and Articles Exploring Sri Krishna.

I dedicate this small book to our Great Souls of Grand Mother, Father and Mother.

MAY WE BE BLESSED BY THEM.

Jayanthinathan, Powai – Mumbai – 400076.

E-Mail: karansank36@gmail.com

Sinkikulam Sri Kailasanathar - Avudai Amman - Malai Bhagavadi Amman

With solemn prayers to our kulatheivam at Sinkikulam (Tirinelveli District) to seek their blessings - Author

PRESENTING MY FIRST COPY OF BOOK - BHAGAVAD GITA SIMPLIFIED AND ARTICLES EXPLORING SRI KRISHNA TO MY EVER-DEDICATED LOVING WIFE VATHSALA

Her Love and Affection Towards Me are Unlimited.
Her Support and Understanding are Unique.
Her Advice and Solution are Priceless.
Her Role as mother is Exemplary.
Her Dedication in Nursing My Bed Ridden Mother is Devotional.

In short, My Wife is Model Wife, Model Mother and Model Daughter-in-Law. As a dutiful husband – though not a model husband – I owe my beloved wife for my successful, happy and religious life.

Sri Bhagavan Krishna is my wife's favourite deity. Because of this, she named our daughter "Meera".

I wholeheartedly present the first printed copy of my book – Bhagavad Gita Simplified and Articles Exploring Sri Krishna - to my ever-loving dutiful wife as a token of my love and affection.

JAI HO VATHSALA!

Thus Thanks Author ....

Sri S. K. Ramanathan:

Two on-line magazines – E-Touch in English for the past 20+ years and Vaaimai in Tamil for the past 16+ years with a limited membership forum of close friends and relatives are being published by me. Sri Ramanathan is one of its readers and contributors and on my request, he volunteered to go through my manuscript of Bhagavad Gita Simplified and Articles Exploring Sri Krishna to enable me to finalise it for printing.

His Profile:

- Retired official from Ministry of Defence Production – Indian Ordinance Factories in 1999.
- Settled at Vellore, Tamandu after retirement.
- Religious and performs ritualistic duties daily.
- He and his wife are ardent devotees of Sri Vidya.
- Interested in reading religious books.
- Interested in sports and watching sports programmes in TV.
- His motto in life: Loka Samastha Sukhino Bhavanthu (Let All Beings in the World Be Happy).

His observations:

I have gone through your manuscript. First, I had a glance through all the pages and next went through in detail, subject wise, which you had written.

First of all, I would like to place my appreciation for the good attempt you had made on this sacred book Bhagavad Gita. I could see the number of books you have referred to, in compiling these details; It is a tremendous effort on your part. Also, I could see you have taken painstaking efforts in collecting as much details as possible subject wise, which is spread over in many chapters. That goes to prove your in-depth study of Gita, if I may say so.

Normally I read Gita slokas with English or Tamil meaning. For a change, I went through your manuscript, out and out in English well written without doubt.

I have two points to make:

1. Somehow, I felt the continuity normally we get, is not there in the manuscript, may be, because the sacred book has been presented subject wise by you.

2. In many places, it is mentioned Arjuna said and Krishna said. Will it be better to write as Arjuna asked or queried and Sri Krishna answered, replied or clarified, as it may be more appropriate. @@

While reading certain English translations, I am reminded of the corresponding famous stanzas, for instance,

Quote: "With devotion – even if one offers Lord Krishna a leaf, a flower, a fruit and water, Sri Krishna accepts it with joy".

पत्रं पुष्पं फलं तोयं यो मे भक्त्या प्रयच्छति ।

तदहं भक्त्युपहृतमश्नामि प्रयतात्मनः ॥ ९-२६ ॥ ....

Similarly, it would have been better if we give reference to the particular stanza in Gita viz chapter and stanza no. so that the readers would be able to relate the thoughts better.

Some years back. I had a chance to listen to Swamiji Dayananda Saraswathi's lectures on Gita - chapter 2.

While giving an introductory speech, he mentioned, the sum and substance of Gita is "TO DO OUR DUTY". To confirm this, he referred to the first stanza in Gita and the last Stanza in Gita – mentioned words of Dharma and mama respectively.

First stanza:

धर्मक्षेत्रे कुरुक्षेत्रे समवेता युयुत्सवः |

मामकाः पाण्डवाश्चैव किमकुर्वत सञ्जय ....(.refer dharma)

The last stanza:

यत्र योगेश्वरः कृष्णो यत्र पार्थो धनुर्धरः।

तत्र श्रीर्विजयो भूतिर्ध्रुवा नीतिर्मतिर्मम॥.........(refer mama)

What is the motto of Bhagavad Gita?

"Perform your duty, you will be taken care " that in nut shell is Gita philosophy. Perform every action with your heart fixed on the Supreme Lord. Renounce attachment to the fruits.

While reading your manuscript, what I felt I am summarising here:

"When we eat, we have rice and supplements like "sambar, rasam, payasam, more" etc with side dishes like koottu, poriyal, appalam etc.

While reading the manuscript in English, I was feeling that I have been served with supplements and side dishes but the main food is missing. This might have been due to your choosing to present Bhagavad

Gita subject wise. Further it seems that you have chosen this method keeping in mind people not knowing Sanskrit. By these observations, it does not mean that in no case I am belittling your efforts.

While talking about of fruits of actions, I remember to have studied somewhere that Vyasa Bhagavan advising Sukar to go and see how King Dasaratha is performing his duties without attachments and learn from him the approach and method of adopting that technique for his own betterment.

Incidentally, I like to mention that the following topics have been well covered and nicely explained: Maya, Comparison of sanyasa, yogi and tyagi, Action – no action – inaction, meditation and praanayaama.

Further, conversation between reader and devotee and critic is interesting to read. Questions by Arjuna and Sri Krishna's elaborate answers have been well brought out in an eye-catching manner separately. Three dolls example is interesting, as mentioned while explaining yoga.

Lot of efforts were taken to collect the various names of Sri Krishna and Arjuna, how many questions Arjuna asked and how Sri Krishna explained, answered or clarified and the list of similes.

I appreciate your good gesture of presenting the first copy of this book to your wife.

It is said:

" यत्र नार्यस्तु पूज्यन्ते रमन्ते तत्र देवताः ।

यत्रैतास्तु न पूज्यन्ते सर्वास्तत्राफलाः क्रियाः ॥ मनुस्मृति ३/५६ ॥

Where women are worshiped, there lives the Gods. Wherever they are not worshiped, all actions result in failure."

May God bless both of you and your family members.

There are some repetitions, maybe they are incidental to the presentation dealt with keeping subject matter as the core of the book. &&&

Finally, I would say it is a good manuscript of Gita in English bringing out most of the good things mentioned in the sacred book.

Author:

@@ Refer his comments above - In Bhagavad Gita the word – uvaca (said) is used throughout and I followed the same. Still, his suggestion to use other words is implemented.

&&& Refer his comments above – Repetitions are removed to the extent possible.

THUS SPEAKS AUTHOR ...

In Gita Dhyana sloka, importance of Bhagavad Gita has been explained thus: "All Upanishads are cows, Sri Krishna is milker, Partha is calf, men of intelligence are drinkers of milk and milk is supreme nectar of Gita."

There is one more sloka which is equally worth quoting and translated sloka runs thus: "Battle of Kurushetra is like a river with Bhima and Drona as banks. Water is Jayadratha. Blue water lily in the river is prince of Gandhara. Crocodile is Salya. Current in the river is Kripa and high wave is Karna. Asvathama and Vikarna are terrible sharks. Duryodhana is whirl-pool. River of battle was crossed by Pandavas because they had Sri Krishna as their ferryman."

There is one familiar and famous explanation in Gita as an extension of symbolism of chariot described in Kathopanisad: "Human body is compared to chariot, in which soul of man is seated as master of chariot with Intellect as charioteer. The mind constitutes reins, and horses are senses. The chariot is coursing through battle field of life. Stationed in the battle field, the bewildered spirit of man represented by Arjuna occupying chariot of the body, looks to the charioteer Sri Krishna, for advice, guidance and inspiration."

Gita is eternal dialogue going on between ego and higher mind in the personality of man struggling in the battlefield of life.

As stated above, Bhagavad Gita is the ultimate Supreme Nectar. Hence, the bare text of Bhagavad Gita themselves is radiant with eternal truths for all to contemplate and to get peace and bliss.

Simplified Bare Text Bhagavad Gita and Articles Exploring Sri Krishna are presented to the readers in all humility by the author – as an ardent devotee of Sri Krishna.

Let there be Light, Let there be Happiness and Let there be Peace.
Let all be blessed by Sri Krishna.

Author: **Jayanthinathan**

Introduction:

Main aim is to make a simple and precise presentation of Bhagavad Gita – its bare text so that it will create interest to read original text.

Text of Bhagavad Gita has been clubbed according to subject matters. This will enable reader to understand it in a better way.

Entire Bhagavad Gita has been divided into four parts for convenient presentation.

Part 1: (1) Arjuna's Dilemma
(2) Yoga of Knowledge
(3) Yoga of Action
(Note: This part covers mostly chapters 1,2,3 & 7)

Part 2: (4) Yoga of Renunciation
(5) Yoga of Devotion
(6) Vedic Rites and Sacrifices
(Note: This part covers mostly chapters 4,5,12, parts of chapters 6 & 18).

Part 3: (7) Techniques of Meditation

(8) Mind, Senses and Lust

(9) Three Gunas – Sattva, Rajas and Tamas

(10) Two Types of Men: Divine and Demonic

(Note: This part covers mostly chapters 14,16 and 17, part of chapters 6 and 18).

Part 4: (11) Theory of Creation.

(12) To Know All About Sri Krishna

(Note: This part covers mostly chapters 7 to 11,13 and 15, parts of chapter 4).

Thus Author Acknowledges...

The listed following sources were very much helpful in writing this book. Pocket Editions of Bare Text of Bhagavad Gita in English versions published by Gita Press, Gorakhpur, by Sri Ramakrishna Math (Translation by Swami Tapasyananda), by Swami Vireswarananda and another one by Swami Chidbhavananda were frequently referred to by me in preparing manuscript for the book.

American Gita Society web page: www.gita-society.com and Web Site of Tapasnyananda https://www.holy-bhagavad-gita.org/ also browsed by me quite often to get clarifications and also to clear doubts. That did not mean that other sources were less valuable and frequented less.

I owe to these sources in accomplishing my holy task of bringing this book.

Last but not the least, I thank Taneesha Publishers who quoted an affordable cost encouraging me to print.

As a mark of my wholehearted acknowledgement of thanks to one and all, I present with all humility, love and affection
a bouquet jointly to all.

LET ALL BE BLESSED
BY BHAGAVAN SRI KRISHNA.

JAI HO ALL

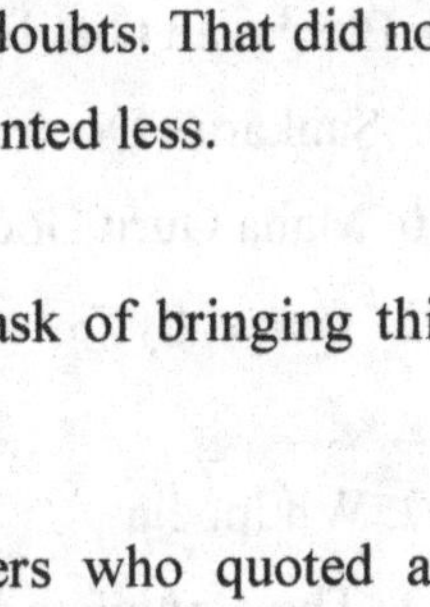

Acknowledgements:

1. American Gita Society web page: www.gita-society.com
2. Srimad Bhagavad Gita by Swami Chidbhavananthar (Tamil & English).
3. Srimad Bhagavad Gita by Swami Tapasyananda (Book) and his web site - https://www.holy-bhagavad-gita.org/
4. Bhagavad Gita by Gita Press, Gorakhpur.
5. Bhagavad Gita by Maha Kavi Subramanya Bharathiyar (Tamil).
6. Discourses of Gita by Vinobaji (Tamil).
7. Bhagavad Gita by Dr. K.K.Ramalingam (Tamil).
8. Bhagavad Gita by M.K. Gandhi.
9. Sankara's Doctrine of Maya by Harry Oldmeadow
10. Maha Guru Google Search Engine
11. Geeta by Swami Chinmayananda - https://shlokam.org/bhagavad-gita/4-13/
12. Wikipedia
13. The Complete Works of Swami Vivekananda published by Advaita Ashrama, Calcutta.

SECTION 1: BHAGAVAD GITA SIMPLIFIED

Bhagavad Gita - Part 1

1. ARJUNA'S DILEMMA

Arjuna: I will not fight!

Arjuna requested Sri Krishna to place the chariot between the armies of Kouravas and Pandavas in the battlefield of Kurukshetra. Arjuna saw his kinsmen and venerable teachers arrayed to fight with him and became sad on seeing them.

Arjuna was afflicted with a dilemma. Arjuna's dilemma in the battle field was due to the sin that would befall him on killing his kinsmen and venerable teachers. He thought that it would be better to be killed by sons of Dhritarashtra than he killing them. Arjuna had gone to the extent of declaring that he would live on alms rather than to slay those noble men. With tears in his eyes, Arjuna sat on the chariot casting aside his bow and arrows.

Arjuna proclaimed: "I will not fight."

Sri Krishna's Advice to Arjuna:

Sri Krishna's advice to Arjuna to shake off his weakness and to get up to fight was not acceptable to Arjuna.

Sri Krishna reasoned with Arjuna thus: "For a warrior like you, it is a great opportunity to fight. By not fighting, you will fail in your duty, lose your reputation and incur sin. Above all, dishonour which is worse than death, will befall you. If killed, you will go to heaven. If won, you will enjoy the kingdom on the earth."

Sri Krishna added the most powerful philosophical reasons like soul exists forever and for that very reason wise men neither grieve for the living nor for the dead, and soul simply acquires another body after death – just like discarding torn garments to wear new ones.

Sri Krishna is the doer

For Arjuna's dilemma about incurring sin, Sri Krishna had this to say: "You fight treating alike victory and defeat, gain and loss, pleasure and pain. Then, you do not incur sin by your performance of mere bodily actions. Above all, if you renounce all dharmas and take refuge in Me, I shall liberate you from all sins. By this surrender of all actions to Me, with your thoughts resting on Me, you are cured yourself of mental confusions and dilemma as well. Kill Drona and Bhisma and Jayadratha and Karna and even other brave warriors. Know that they stand already killed by Me. Hence, no sin for you and you will surely conquer the enemies."

Sri Krishna also explained that all actions are performed only by human qualities (gunas) of Nature (Prakriti). But due to egoism, man thinks "I am the doer". The forces of nature with the aid of human organs as their instruments of actions are responsible for the performance of work. The person who knows the truth about this role of the forces of Nature in getting work done do not become attached to the work.

Sri Krishna was more emphatic in His reasoning when He said: "Non-egoists are not tainted by the actions – even killing will not bind them. Filled with egoism, you think, 'I will not fight'. This is vain on your part. Your resolve and your nature as Kshatriya will compel you to fight. You are controlled by your own nature. Therefore, you will do – even against your will – what you do not wish to do out of delusion."

Arjuna: I will fight

Finally, Sri Krishna had this to say to Arjuna as a warning: "You abide in this teaching of Mine, full of faith and free from trivial objections. This also releases you from bondage of all actions. If anyone finds fault with My teachings and fail to act thereon due to delusion, he is sure to be ruined. He who is ignorant, wanting in faith and of a doubting mind, is ruined.

For doubting man, there is neither this world nor other world, nor happiness. Therefore, O Arjuna, this doubt in your heart was born of ignorance. Destroy this doubt to pieces with the sword of knowledge. Establish yourself in karma yoga and arise."

Again, Sri Krishna asked Arjuna: Have all delusions born of ignorance been dispelled from you?

Arjuna confirmed: My delusions are destroyed. I have regained my wisdom through your grace. I now stand firm, with all my doubts cleared, ready to act according to your solemn advices.

Now, I will fight.

2. Yoga of Knowledge

Knowledge of soul

There are two souls – human soul and supreme soul. Learning and knowing about these two souls are called yoga of knowledge.

First lesson to know about souls is to know that souls are invisible to our physical eyes before birth and death, though visible between birth and death. Another important factor about souls is that even though body is slain, soul is not. Soul neither kills nor is killed. Soul cannot be cut, burned, wetted or dried. As a corollary, it is eternal, everlasting and omnipresent. Still, soul is looked upon as an object of wonder and only very few know what soul is.

Results of yoga of knowledge

One can know true nature of yoga of knowledge only by becoming a disciple of seers. One needs to prostrate at their feet, render them services and question them with an open and guiltless heart. Then those wise seers of truth will instruct him in that knowledge. He becomes enlightened and ignorance will delude him no more. Now, he will see the entire creation first within his own self, and then in Sri Krishna. Due to his enlightenment, all his sins are burnt to ashes, as a blazing fire burns fuel to ashes. Such a person becomes a sage – purified soul by his knowledge. He becomes embodiment of faith, zeal and self-control. In that state, he attains supreme peace.

3. Yoga of Selfless Action

Characteristics of Yoga of Action

Action without attachment to its fruits is selfless action and this is called Yoga of Action or Karma Yoga. Greatness of yoga of action is that even if action is left incomplete, one is not faced with any adverse effect. Further such selfless action saves performer from great fear of birth and death.

Actions of great men become standards for ordinary men to follow. Hence such great men need to do duty to the best of their abilities with mind attached to Sri Krishna. Success and failure will not affect such great men and they are free from both virtue and vice.

A prolonged practice of Karma Yoga is necessary to attain purity of heart. Attainment of purity of heart will light up truth in the self in course of time. This brings peace and control of mind. Others, working under sway of desires, are attached to the fruits of actions and get bound.

If one is content with pair of opposites like pleasure and pain, gain and loss, victory and defeat, heat and cold, he is not bound by action. This contentment is achieved by performing actions as offerings to God and without attachment. Then, bondages of all his actions melt away and he becomes a Karma Yogi.

One is not touched by sin, as a lotus leaf by water, if he performs actions dedicating them to Sri Krishna and giving up attachment and free from fear and anger. Such person is purified by the penance of wisdom. He becomes one with Sri Krishna.

Though actions with attachment are unwise acts, for maintenance of world order, wise man acts without attachment. Such enlightened man should not cause confusion in the minds of ignorant people by his conduct - giving an impression of 'non-action' to 'his unattached action.' He should make people interested in all activities.

Janaka and other wise men reached perfection through action without attachment alone.

Power in detachment from fruits of action is that the performer of action is freed from the action itself. Motive force of action should not be fruits of action.

Non-attachment to fruits of action should not lead into inaction. One who works only to enjoy fruits of his labour, is verily unhappy because one has no control over fruits of action. Fruits of action can be renounced through Yoga of Knowledge. Having all doubts destroyed by knowledge and becoming self-possessed, such person is not bound by action.

Action is Superior to Inaction

Arjuna asked: If you consider knowledge as superior to action, why then do you urge me to this dreadful action? By seemingly conflicting words, you are confusing my mind. Tell me only about that which definitely leads to my highest good.

Sri Krishna explained: Freedom from bondage of action is not attained by merely abstaining from action. No one can remain inactive even for a moment. Everyone is driven to action by forces of Nature. He who controls all sense organs but dwells in his mind on the objects of senses, deceives himself. But if a person excels by controlling sense organs by power of the will and at the same time engaging in organs of action, he attains the status of a yogi in action.

Therefore, perform your allotted duty. For, action is superior to inaction. By desisting from action, you cannot even maintain your body.

Sri Krishna as Lord of Action

Sacrificial duty keeps wheel of creation in motion. Those who rejoice in sense pleasure with no sacrificial duties, are said to lead vain and sinful lives.

If anyone is delighted, contented and satisfied in the self, then for such enlightened person, there is no loss by his inaction. Because he does not depend on anybody for anything.

Sri Krishna said that there was nothing in all the three worlds – heaven, earth and lower regions, for Him to do, nor was there anything worth attaining by Him, yet He continued to work. The reasons for Sri Krishna's continuous non-stop work are explained by Himself as follows: "If I do not engage in action relentlessly, people would follow My path resulting in destruction of the worlds. Then, I should be the cause of confusion among men and of their ultimate destruction. I am therefore the Lord of Action."

Prescribed Action

Even ancient seeker for liberation performed actions. Therefore, one needs to perform such actions as have been done by those ancient seekers.

Many types of spiritual disciplines for action of body, mind and senses are described in Vedas. Thus, knowing truth about spiritual disciplines and also through their performance, one shall be freed from bondage of action and also from evil effects of birth and death.

Soul in the body- the embodied soul is action less. Non-participant soul in the body is witness for the action of the body.

Bhagavad Gita – Part 2

4. Yoga of Renunciation

Karma Yoga is superior to Sanyasa Yoga

Arjuna questioned: You praise in one breath both renunciation of action (Sanyasa) and performance of action (Karma Yoga). Tell me definitely, which one is better of the two.

Sri Krishna said: Of the two, performance of action is superior to renunciation of action. Because renunciation of action (sanyasa) is difficult to practise compared to performance of action (karma yoga or selfless action). But renunciation and performance of action - both lead to liberation. But man of selfless action (karma yogi) by keeping his mind fixed on God, reaches Brahman faster than a Sanyasi.

In fact, only ignorant treats yoga of knowledge and yoga of action as different. But wise knows that yoga of knowledge and action are same. It is because the person, who has truly mastered one, gets the benefits of both. State, which one attains by knowledge, is attained by selfless action too. He, who sees both knowledge and selfless action as one, sees truly.

Sanyasi is Yogi

Embodied soul renounces all actions through its control of mind. And then soul rests at ease in the city of nine gates of the body - two eyes, two nostrils, two ears, one mouth, the anus and the genitals. Such self-realised soul neither acts nor causes to act.

A perpetual renouncer of action neither dislikes nor desires. Such Renouncer does his duty without caring for fruits of action. One does not become a sanyasi (renouncer) merely by not lighting sacred fire and one does not become a yogi merely by abstaining from work.

Renunciation (sanyasa) is same as selfless action (karma yoga). Selfless action is means to attain the heights of yoga. Once one has reached that stage, self-realisation leads to peace of mind. At that stage, one ceases to have any attachment either for objects of senses or for actions. Hence, a karma yogi renounces selfish motive behind an action. Renouncer (Sanyasi) is also a Yogi.

Renunciation (Sanyasa) and Relinquishment (Tyaga)

Arjuna requested: I desire to know the true nature of renunciation (sanyasa) and relinquishment (tyaga) and the difference between the two.

Sri Krishna explained: Renunciation (sanyasa) is abandonment of all desires and result-oriented actions. Relinquishment (Tyaga) is abandonment of fruits of all actions. Abandonment of fruits of **ritualistic actions** to achieve specific rewards alone is laid down for a sanyasi, leaving ascetic actions untouched. But, Tyaga covers abandonment of fruits of **all actions**. In short, sanyasa is tyaga, but tyaga is not sanyasa.

Liberation through Abandonment of Fruits of Action

Some sages declare that all actions should be given up as evil. Some other sages say that sacrifice (yajna), gift and austerity should not be abandoned. Those other sages argue that sacrifice, gift and austerity are obligatory duties and hence they should not be abandoned because these obligatory duties are beneficial to the world at large.

Abandonment of the obligatory duties out of delusion is Ignorance (Tamasika). Abandonment due to fear of body pains is Passion (Rajasika).

Abandonment of fruits of action is Goodness (Sattvika).

Relinquisher (Tyagi) does not distinguish between agreeable and disagreeable work. For embodied being, it is impossible to renounce action completely. Only feasibility is to renounce attachment to the fruits of actions and such being is considered relinquisher (Tyagi).

What are the fruits of actions?

The fruits of actions consist of three characteristics - evil, good and mixed. These threefold effects of actions will never accrue to the relinquisher.

Abandonment of fruits in all works will fetch liberation, which leads to Sri Krishna.

5. Yoga of Devotion

Worship of Divine Forms and Formless:

Arjuna said: Some Devotees worship you in your Divine Form and some others worship you in your Formless Absolute. Of these, who is the best knower of Yoga?

Sri Krishna answered: Those who worship me in my Divine Form are the best yogis. Those who worship me in my formless Absolute – with their senses controlled, even-minded and devoted to welfare of all, also come to Me. But obstacles faced by worshipers of Formless Absolute are far greater because comprehension of formless Supreme by embodied beings is very difficult. On the other hand, those who meditate on Me in my divine form as their sole refuge, are lifted by Me from the ocean of death-bound worldly existence.

If you are unable to fix the mind on Me in spite of repeated practices, then devote yourself whole-heartedly to works of service to Me abandoning fruits of action with self-subdued.

Hence, it should be understood that knowledge is better than action, meditation is better than knowledge, and renunciation of fruits of action is better than meditation.

Peace immediately follows renunciation.

Prayers:

People worship Sri Krishna with different motives and desires and Sri Krishna fulfils their prayers.

Four types of virtuous men worship Sri Krishna:

1. Man in distress,
2. Man seeking knowledge

3. Man seeking wealth
4. Man seeking wisdom.

Of these, man seeking wisdom, ever steadfast and devoted to Sri Krishna is the best.

All the four are noble but Sri Krishna regards the wise man – the enlightened devotee as His very Self. It is because the one who is steadfast in mind abides in His Supreme Abode. At the end of many births, man of wisdom takes refuge in Sri Krishna, realizing that Sri Krishna is all. A great soul of that type is rare to find.

Others, however, adore other deities with various forms of worship pertaining to them. Still, they do get their desires fulfilled, which are ordained by Sri Krishna.

With devotion – even if one offers Sri Krishna a leaf, a flower, a fruit and water, Sri Krishna accepts it with joy. First offer them to Sri Krishna – whether it is food, sacrifice, charity or austerity. Then only, one will be freed from the bonds of work.

Real Knowledge is to know Sri Krishna who will release embodied souls from miseries of material existence. Though the mighty wind blows everywhere, it rests always in the sky. Likewise, all living souls always rest in Sri Krishna.

Who is the devotee dear to Sri Krishna?

Devotee of Sri Krishna hates no being. He is friendly and compassionate to all. He is same to friend and foe and also in honour and dishonour. He is free from the feeling of 'I and Mine', even-minded in cold, heat, pain and pleasure and forgiving. He is ever content, steady in self-meditation, and possessed of firm conviction, with mind and intellect fixed on Sri Krishna. Such a devotee is dear to Sri Krishna.

Devotee of Sri Krishna causes fear to none. At the same time, none can frighten him. He is free from joy, anger, fear and anxiety. Such a devotee is dear to Sri Krishna.

Devotee of Sri Krishna is desire-less, pure, resourceful, unattached, unworried and selfless in all his undertakings. Such a devotee is dear to Sri Krishna.

Devotee of Sri Krishna neither rejoices nor grieves nor hates nor desires, renouncing good and evil, full of devotion. Such a devotee is dear to Sri Krishna.

Devotee of Sri Krishna is free from attachment. He is indifferent to censure or praise. He is quiet, content with anything, homeless, steady-minded. Such a devotee is dear to Sri Krishna.

Devotee of Sri Krishna follows virtuous path to Immortality with devotion, looking upon Sri Krishna as Supreme Goal. Such a devotee is dear to Sri Krishna.

6. Vedic Rites and Sacrifices (Yajna)

Vedic Rites

To think, as if there is nothing else in Vedas except rituals for the sole purpose of obtaining heavenly enjoyment is a misconception. Real purpose of Vedas lies not in the delight of melodious chanting of Vedas.

Rituals of Vedas are dominated by material desires and attainment of heaven as the highest goal of life. Such specific rites may attain prosperity and enjoyment. But rebirth is the result of their actions. Such ritualistic activities do not lead to self-realization, as their minds are attached to pleasure and power, obscuring their judgement of the ultimate goal.

Limitation of Vedas

Vedas deal with three modes of human qualities (gunas) – viz. goodness, passion and ignorance (sattva, raja and tama). One should also rise above these modes of human characters to become self-conscious. One should be ever balanced and unconcerned with the thoughts of acquisition and preservation.

When huge lake water becomes available, then usage of well water is limited. Similarly, Vedas are of limited use for self-realised person. When intellect is confused by conflicting opinions and ritualistic doctrine of Vedas, then one needs to concentrate on Supreme Being. Then the intellect shall stay steady and firm.

Sacrifices (Yajna)

There are various forms of sacrifices with different offerings. Some yogis perform service of worship to celestial controllers, while others study scriptures for self- knowledge. Some restrain their senses and give up their sensual pleasures. Others perform breathing and other yogic exercises. Some give charity and offer their wealth as a sacrifice. Others restrict their diet and do meditation. All of them have their sins consumed away by sacrifice and also understand the meaning of sacrificial worship.

They obtain the nectar of self-knowledge as a result of their sacrifice and attain Supreme Self. For those who do not perform sacrifices, even this world is not a happy place, how can the other world be?

Sacrifice through knowledge is superior to sacrifice performed with material things.

Bhagvad Gita - Part 3

7. Meditation

Techniques of Meditation : A yogi is to sit in solitude in a clean place. His seat shall be neither too high nor too low. The seat is to be made up of the kusa grass, a deerskin and a cloth spread one over the other. He shall hold body, head and neck erect and gazing at the tip of his nose without looking around. He shall sit absorbed in Sri Krishna.

Yoga is not possible for one who eats too much or for him who eats too little; it is also not for those who sleep too much or too little.

Yogi's Mind is Abode of Sri Krishna. Practice of Yoga ensures self-purification which will lead to everlasting peace of mind. Yogi's Mind should be always be pure to have Sri Krishna to reside in it permanently.

To achieve this, Yogi restrains his thinking faculty and senses. Yoga helps to constantly control the mind to be free from desires and possessions thereby ensuring its purity.

Senses are mastered by meditation. Meditation brings senses under control and fixes mind firmly on God.

Practice of Yoga ensures Tranquillity and One Pointed Mind which are requisite for its purity.

Yoga is the destroyer of desire, pain and sin. Peace of mind alone through Yoga will lead to supreme bliss. One feels infinite bliss that is perceivable only through intellect, and is beyond the reach of the senses.

After realizing Absolute Reality, one is never separated from it. Disciplined mind of a yogi practising meditation is like a lamp in a windless place that does not flicker. Such a yogi succeeds in overcoming restless and unsteady mind from all those objects after which it runs. Yogi thus brings back his mind to the reflection of God.

To Reach Sri Krishna through Meditation

One is fit for becoming Brahman, if the person is endowed with pure understanding. He has to restrain self with firmness abandoning attraction and aversion. He dwells in solitude, eats but little and with his speech, body and mind subdued. He always engages in meditation and concentration. He abandons egoism, violence, arrogance, desire, enmity, property. He is free from the notion of "mine" and he is peaceful. He becomes serene-minded and neither grieves nor desires. He is same to all beings and obtains supreme devotion of Sri Krishna. By devotion one truly understands what and who Sri Krishna is in essence. Having known Sri Krishna in essence, one immediately merges with Sri Krishna.

Restraining all gates of body and fixing mind in heart region, and then drawing life-breath to head, one should get established in steadfast yogic concentration.

In short, meditation is: Shutting out external sense-objects, fixing the gaze between eyebrows, controlling outgoing and incoming breaths that move through nostrils, with senses, mind and intellect restrained, and free from desire, fear and anger.

Fate of those who failed in Yoga

Arjuna said: O, Lord Krishna! You have said that yoga of meditation is characterized by peace of mind, but due to restlessness of mind, I do not perceive steady state of mind. Mind is very restless, turbulent, and obstinate. It is hard to control as wind.

Lord Krishna answered: It is hard to control restless mind. But mind can be controlled by practice of meditation and by non-attachment. If one can subdue mind and having attained full control by striving through proper means, he becomes a yogi and I am sure of it.

Arjuna asked: What is the fate of a man who, though endowed with a firm faith, is not steadfast in his practices owing to distractions, and therefore fails to reach spiritual perfection? Do they not perish like a dispersing cloud having lost both heavenly and worldly pleasures, support-less and bewildered on the path of self-realization? This doubt of mine, you should dispel in its entirety, for there is none else but you who can remove this doubt?

Lord Krishna clarified: Doer of good never comes to grief. There is no fall for him either here or hereafter. Successful yogi goes to heaven to which men of meritorious deeds are entitled. Having resided there for countless years, such yogi's soul takes birth in the house of pious and wealthy man. Failed yogi, however, does not go to heaven, but is born in the family of enlightened man. Then he regains the knowledge acquired in his former birth and he strives more than before for perfection. The one, who takes birth in such a family, is carried towards Me by virtue of yogic practices of previous life. Even the inquirer of yoga is superior to those who perform Vedic rituals.

Yogi is purified from sins and perfected through many births and then, reaches supreme goal. Yogi is superior to ascetics; he is regarded as superior to men of knowledge and greater also than those ritualists. Therefore, O Arjuna, be a yogi.

8. Mind, Senses and Lust:

Mind & Senses

Diverse modes of mind are seen in all beings and they proceed from Sri Krishna alone. Diverse modes of mind are as follows: Intelligence, knowledge, sanity, patience, truth, sense-control, mind-control, pleasure, pain, birth, death, fear, fearlessness, non-injury, equanimity, contentment, austerity, charity and fame.

One must elevate – and not degrade – oneself by one's own mind.

Mind alone is one's friend or enemy. Mind is friend to those who have control over it, and mind acts like an enemy to those who do not control it. But mind of yogi is satisfied with knowledge and realization. Yogi is unperturbed and has senses under his control.

For yogi, a clod of earth, a stone and a gold are same – not affected by its forms or its values. Similarly, such yogi looks equally on a well - wisher, a friend, an enemy, a neutral, an arbiter, a hateful person, a relative, a good or a sinful person.

Lust

Arjuna asked: Impelled by what, does man commit sin even against his will?

Sri Krishna explained: It is lust born out of passion (Rajoguna) that becomes anger, when unfulfilled. Lust is insatiable and is a great devil. Lust is known as eternal enemy of wise here on earth. As the fire is covered by smoke, as a mirror by dust and as an embryo by the womb, so self-knowledge gets covered by different degrees of this insatiable fire of lust.

Abode of lust is senses, mind and intellect; lust veils knowledge and deludes embodied soul. Therefore, control senses at the beginning itself. Slay this foul enemy of lust - the destroyer of all knowledge and realisation.

Senses are said to be greater than body; but greater than senses are mind. Greater than mind is intellect; and what is greater than intellect is soul. Lust is a mighty energy, which is killed by the weapon of spiritual practices.

Spiritual practices are achieved by controlling mind by intellect.

Mark of the man of steadfast wisdom

Mind of the man of steadfast wisdom is unperturbed by sorrow. He does not crave pleasures. He is completely free from passion, fear and anger. He neither rejoices nor recoils on meeting with good and evil.

Such a person of steadfast wisdom can completely withdraw senses from sense objects, as a tortoise withdraws its limbs into the shell for protection from calamity.

Restless senses forcibly carry away mind of even a wise person striving for perfection. Desires for sensual pleasures fades away, if one abstains from sense enjoyment, but the craving for sense enjoyment remains in a very subtle form. This subtle craving also completely disappears in the case of man of stable mind, when he sees Supreme Self.

Man dwelling on sense objects develops attachment for them; from attachment springs up desire, and from desire ensues anger. From anger arises passion; from passion, confusion of memory; from confusion of memory, loss of reason; and from loss of reason, one goes to complete ruin.

But, a disciplined person, enjoying sense objects with senses under control and free from attachments and aversions, attains tranquillity.

Tranquillity destroys all sorrows. Intellect of such a tranquil person becomes completely steady and united with supreme.

One who has not controlled his mind and senses cannot think of God and hence he can have no peace.

How can there be happiness for one lacking peace of mind?

A storm takes away a boat on the sea from its destination. Similarly, mind is tossed by storm of roving senses, deluding intellect – moving mind away from shore of peace and happiness.

River waters enter full ocean without creating any disturbance. In the same way, desires do not create any disturbance in the mind of steadfast man, but his desires dissipate.

Heat and cold, pain and pleasure are due to contacts of senses with their sense objects. They come and go and are impermanent. Man of steadfast wisdom is balanced in pain and pleasure and is fit for immortality

All beings follow their nature. Even wise act according to their own nature.

What, then, is value of sense restraint?

Value of sense restraint is self-realisation. Attraction and repulsion are rooted in all sense objects. These are to be controlled, as they are two principal enemies standing in the way of self-realisation.

9. Three Types of Human Nature: (Three Gunas – Sattva, Rajas, Tamas)

Three Gunas

Nature- consisting of five basic elements – air, fire, water, earth and ether – are mother of all creations, while seed-giving father is Supreme Self. All beings are created from union of matter or body and Supreme Self, which is in the form of spirit or soul. Factors that bind soul to body are threefold human characters (three gunas) – viz. sattva - goodness, raja -passion and tama – ignorance.

Sattva Mode or Goodness mode - pure and luminous, binds soul to body and it moves soul upwards and it keeps soul at the top. It is most beneficial to soul to reach heaven.

Raja Mode or Passion mode – cupidity and attachment- binds soul to body with actions and their fruits. It keeps soul in the middle with the onslaughts of greed, selfish works, restlessness and excitement. Such soul, while leaving the body, is reborn among those attached to action.

Tama Mode or Ignorant Mode – Impure and filled with Delusion – binds soul to body with carelessness, laziness and sleep. It keeps soul at the bottom. Such soul while leaving the body is reborn as lower creatures.

All actions are due to these three modes of human nature functioning as the agents of actions.

Soul conquering these human qualities attains to Supreme State. When one rises above these characteristic modes of material nature that originate in the body, attains immortality or salvation and is freed from the pains of birth, old age and death.

Types of Human Character

Three types of human character (Gunas) are moulded by the nature of faith, food, sacrifice, austerity and gifts.

Sattva Guna :

Faith of Person in the mode of goodness makes him to worship God. He likes **foods** that promote longevity, virtue, strength, health, happiness and joy and such foods are juicy, soft, nourishing and agreeable. He performs **sacrifice** as enjoined by the scriptures without attachment for the fruits, with mind fixed on the service only. He performs **Austerity** without any desire for the fruit. He gives **gifts** out of a sheer sense of duty, without expectation of any kind of return, at the proper time and place, to a fit recipient.

Raja Guna:

Faith of person in the mode of Passion makes him to worship demi-god and demons. As for **foods**, he likes foods that are bitter, sour, salty, excessively heating, pungent, dry and burning and that cause pain, grief and disease. His **sacrifice** is performed in expectation of reward or for self-glorification. His mode of **austerity** is for gaining respect, honour and reverence. He gives **gifts** with a view to receive in return, or looking for the fruit, or again grudgingly.

Tama Guna:

Faith of person in the mode of Ignorance makes him to worship the dead and the groups of ghosts. His **food** is stale, tasteless, stinking, cooked overnight, refuse and impure. He performs **sacrifice** without following the scripture and without food and mantra. His **austerity** is performed with a foolish obstinacy, with self-torture or for the purpose of destroying another. His **Gift** is given at a wrong place or time, to unworthy persons, without respect or with insult.

Knowledge, Action, Actor, Agent, Intellect, Firmness and Happiness of three gunas

Human qualities - three gunas are moulded by the specific nature of knowledge, action, actor, agent, intellect, firmness and happiness.

Sattva Guna:

Person in the mode of **goodness** has **knowledge** by which he sees a single Imperishable Being in all existences as undivided in the divided. Such person's **action** is free from attachment, love or hatred and non-desirous of the fruit. Such person's **agent or doer** is free from attachment, non-egoistic, endued with firmness and zeal and unaffected by success or failure. Such person's **intellect** is that by which one knows the path of work and renunciation, right and wrong action, fear and fearlessness, bondage and liberation. Such person's **firmness** is regulated by yoga of meditation. Such person's **happiness** is pleasure that appears as poison in the beginning, but turning to nectar in the end.

Raja Guna:

Person in the mode of **Passion** has the **knowledge** by which he sees different entities of different kinds as varying from one another. Such person's **action** is done out of desires and egoism. Such person's **agent** is one who is passionate, desiring to obtain fruit of action, greedy, cruel, impure, moved by joy and sorrow. His **intellect** is that by which one makes a distorted grasp of dharma and adharma and right and wrong action. His **firmness** is action with attachment and for the fruits. Such person's **happiness** is pleasure that appears as nectar in the beginning, but turning to poison in the end.

Tama Guna:

Person in the mode of **Ignorance** has the **knowledge** by which one clings to the body as if it is all – a view that is irrational and untrue. Such person's **action** is done without caring for the consequence, loss, injury and ability. Such person's **agent** or doer is one who is unsteady, vulgar, stubborn, deceitful, malicious, lazy, depressed, and procrastinating. Such person's **intellect** is that by which one regards adharma as dharma and views all things in a perverted way. Such person's **firmness** is dullness with sleep, fear, grief, despair and conceit. Such person's **happiness** is pleasure that confuses in the beginning and it ends in sleep, laziness and carelessness.

There is no being on earth or in heaven, which can remain free from these three modes of material nature. Duties of human beings are distributed according to the Gunas born of their own nature.

To Conquer Gunas

Sri Krishna explained in detail to Arjuna the marks of those who have succeeded in conquering three-fold human characters.

Sri Krishna said: Senses and mind due to forces of three-fold human characters act and enjoy and not the real self or soul inside the human body. Those who conquered three-fold characters remain unwavering in all situations, self-poised in pleasure and pain. Such persons do not differentiate love and hate. They are also unmoved by praise and blame, by honour and humiliation. Such persons view friends and foes alike and have abandoned all sense of doer ships in all actions.

Such persons serve Sri Krishna through the communion of steadfast devotion and attain fitness to become Supreme Self.

Sri Krishna declares: I am the Supreme Self, Heaven, Eternal Law and Bliss.

Three Kinds of Austerities

Austerities are of three kinds pertaining to body, speech and mind. Austerity of body means body worshiping Gods, teachers and wise. Austerity of speech means speech causing no excitement, truthful, pleasant, beneficial, and practice of sacred recitation.

Austerity of mind means mind of gentleness, silence, self-control and purity of thought.

10. Two Types of Men: Divine and Demonic:

There are two types of men in this world – a divine nature and a demonic nature. Divine nature is for liberation, Demonic nature is for bondage.

Arjuna was born with divine qualities.

Characteristics of Divine nature are: Fearlessness, purity of heart, steadfastness in knowledge and yoga, alms giving, control of the senses, sacrifice, study of scripture, austerity, honesty, non-violence, truth, absence of anger, renunciation, tranquillity, compassion, freedom from greed, gentleness, modesty, forgiveness, purity, absence of hatred, absence of pride.

Characteristics of Demonic nature are: Men possessing demonic nature know not what to do and what to refrain from; neither purity nor right conduct nor truth is found in them.

By forces of lust, pride of power and attachment, persons of demonic nature are performing acts contrary to scriptural injunctions. They torture their own bodies which in turn tortures Sri Krishna dwelling in them.

Food, worship, penance and charity differ as per their gunas.

Demonic Persons say: Universe is unreal. For them, Sexual union of man and woman alone and nothing else causes the world. They consider sense gratification their highest aim and they are convinced that sense pleasure is everything and they strive to obtain wealth by unlawful means.

They are ruined souls of small intellect, of fierce deeds, and rise as the enemies of the world for its destruction. They work with impure motives due to their insatiable desires, hypocrisy, pride and evil ideas.

They say to themselves being deluded by ignorance: "So much wealth is already with me and yet again more wealth shall be mine. That enemy has been slain by me, and I shall slay others also. I am successful, powerful and happy. Who is equal to me? I shall perform sacrifice, I shall give alms, and I shall rejoice."

These malicious people, due to their egoism, power, arrogance, lust and anger, hate Sri Krishna who dwells in their own bodies and those of others.

Sri Krishna hurls these evildoers forever into the wombs of the demons only. Falling into the wombs of demons, in life after life, they go to still lower states of degradation, without attaining Sri Krishna.

Bhagavad Gita - Part 4

11. Theory of Creation:

The Field and The Knower of the Field

The Field (Kshetra) is usually identified with Body. The knower of the Field (Kshetrajna) is identified with Soul or Atma. Knowledge about body and soul is wisdom. This wisdom has been sung by seers in many ways in Vedic hymns and also in verses of Brahmasutras.

The field apart from body has the following properties:

Five (5) elements – viz. fire, water, air, earth and ether; ten organs (10) – viz. five knowledge organs – eyes, ears, nose, tongue and skin and five action organs – legs, hands, mouth, anus and genitals; and five (5) objects of the senses – viz. sight, sound, smell, taste and touch; egoism (1), intellect ((1), mind (1); un-manifested (Primordial Matter) (1).

In short, elements (5), senses and sense objects (15), ego (1), intellect (1), mind (1) and soul (1) totalling in all 24 elements – are major factors of the field of the body.

Hence the field is not merely body but it is a part of the Nature or Prakriti of 24 elements as detailed above.

Sri Krishna declares that Knower of the Field (Kshetrajna) is to be aware of knowledge and Ignorance to ferry Prakriti with its 24 elements towards Supreme Soul – Imperishable though dwelling in the perishable body – unmanifested in the manifested.

Sri Krishna has listed the following characteristics to Kshetrajna as Knowledge and what is contrary is Ignorance:Intelligence, humbleness, modesty, uprightness, non-violence, service of the teacher, purity, steadfastness, self-control, dispassion toward the objects of the senses, absence of egotism, keeping in mind the evils of birth, disease, old age, and death, non-attachment, absence of clinging to spouse, children, home, even-mindedness amidst desired and undesired events in life, constant and exclusive devotion towards Me, an inclination for solitary places and an aversion for mundane society, constancy in spiritual knowledge and philosophical pursuit of the Absolute Truth.

Nature is divided itself into material and spiritual nature. This distinction between Field and Supreme is to be perceived with the eye of wisdom. Due to this wisdom, the deliverance of beings from nature is achieved and then soul reaches Supreme.

Nature (Prakriti) consists of lower and higher elements. Material nature is lower and Spiritual nature is higher. Lower material nature is divided into eightfold – viz. Earth, Water, Fire, Air, Ether (Five Elements), intellect, ego and mind.

Higher nature is only one i.e., soul – life element by which whole universe is sustained.

All creatures have evolved from these twofold natures of Sri Krishna– lower and higher natures as their source.

Sri Krishna is origin and dissolution of whole universe. Everything in universe is strung on Sri Krishna, as rows of gems on a string.

Supreme Self has no beginning and possesses no gunas. It is imperishable and neither acts nor is tainted. As all-pervading ether is not tainted by reason of its subtlety, in the same way self-seated in all bodies is not tainted. As one sun illumines whole world, so the one soul illumines whole field – all human bodies.

Nature, Soul and Gunas

The nature is said to be the cause in the production of the body and senses. Soul is said to be the cause in the experience of pleasure and pain. Soul is seated in the nature and experiences gunas. Attachment to gunas is the cause of birth in good and evil wombs for the souls. Soul dwelling in this body is really the same as Supreme.

Supreme has been spoken of as witness, true guide, sustainer of all, experiencer as the embodied soul. Whoever thus knows soul and nature together with gunas, is never born again. Whatever is born it is due to the union of body and soul.

Yoga of Purushothama

Ashvattha tree or pipal tree or fig tree represents Material World. This tree is imperishable but to be perished at the end of a yuga. This is a strange tree with its roots to the sky instead of to the ground and its trunk and branches down to the earth. It is an upside down tree. One who knows the secret of this tree is the knower of Vedas.

Its leaves are Vedas, buds are sense objects , branches are gunas and roots are actions of men. This strange tree can be be cut by axe of detachment by embodied souls .

Man with axe of detachment having freed from vanity, delusion, desire of senses and beyond the dualities of pleasure and pain by cutting the branches of Asvattha tree becomes a liberated Soul. Many such Liberated Souls find permanent Abode with Lord Krishna at top of Ashvatta tree.

Neither the sun nor the moon, nor fire can illumine Abode of Supreme. Know that radiance of the moon and the brightness of the fire come from Supreme.

Abiding in the body of human beings, soul through Vaishvanara –

meaning fire of digestion with association of Prana and Apana - digests Four types of food.

(Note: Four types of food are: 1. Foods that are chewed, such as bread, chapatti, etc. 2. Liquid or semi-solid foods that are swallowed or drunk such as milk, juice, etc. 3. Foods that are sucked, such as sugarcane. 4. Foods that are licked, such as honey, etc.)

Souls in the world (Purushas) are of two types - Non-Liberated and Liberated.

Sri Krishna is beyond the non-liberated souls and dwells in the liberated souls. Therefore, Sri Krishna in the world and in the Veda is described as 'Purushothama', the highest Purusha or the Supreme Self. Thus, Sri Krishna Himself has imparted this most profound teaching. A true understanding of it makes a man really wise and established in a sense of total fulfilment. Such wise men worship Sri Krishna with all their hearts as Supreme Person.

As the air carries fragrance from place to place, so does the embodied soul carry the mind and senses with it, when it leaves an old body and enters a new one.

Five elements of nature are direct bearing on five sense organs – like the brilliance in fire for the eyes, the taste in water for the mouth, the sweet fragrance in earth for the nose, the sound in ether for the ears and the life in air for the body. Soul enjoys the object of senses, while dwelling in the senses of hearing, sight, touch, taste and smell as well as the mind.

The ignorant knows not the soul - departing from, or dwelling in the body, or enjoying the objects of senses. The Pure only can recognize Atma or soul.

Four Divisions of Society:

Four divisions of human society were created by Sri Krishna based on aptitude and vocation (gunas and karma). Though Sri Krishna is the creator of this system of the division of labour, He is not an agent but the immortal Lord.

Division of labour is based on one's ability to perform. They are Brahmins (Intellectuals) for sacred obligations, Kshatriyas (warriors) for protections, Vaishyas (traders) for business and Shudras (workers) for subordinate services. Perfect performance of one's natural duty itself is worship of Sri Krishna.

One's own duty, though devoid of merit, is preferable to the duty of another well performed. For, even death in doing one's duty leads to one's good, while a duty alien to one's guna is burdened with the fear of downfall.

12. To Know All About Sri Krishna

Sri Krishna's Creation

In the beginning, the Creator (Prajapathi) created human beings together with Vedic sacrifice (Yajna).

After this creation, the Creator said: "By this you propagate. May this be to you the Cow of Plenty (Kamathenu) yielding all your wants! Serve the celestial controllers (Devas) with selfless service and they will bless you with rain and other desired gifts. Thus, by mutual helps, you shall attain the highest good. The celestial controllers will give you all desired objects."

Gifts are to be shared with others. If human beings do not share the gifts with others, they are thieves. By sharing with others, they are freed from all sin.

If one cooks food only for himself, he verily eats sin. All beings are evolved from food; production of food is dependent on rain; rain results from sacrifice, and sacrifice is rooted in prescribed action. Prescribed action has its origin in Vedas, and Vedas proceed from Supreme. Hence Supreme - all-pervading Infinite is always present in sacrifice.

Incarnation or Avatar

Sri Krishna said: Immortal yoga of knowledge and selfless action were taught by me first to Vivaswan (sun god) who, in turn, taught this yoga to Manu – his son and who, in turn, to Ikswaku – son of Manu.

Thus, transmitted in succession from father to son and due to long efflux of time, this yoga decayed in this world. The same ancient yoga which is a supreme secret, has been today imparted to you by Me because you are my devotee and friend.

Arjuna questioned: You were born later, but Vivaswan was born long back in ancient time. How, then, am I to believe that you taught this yoga at the beginning of creation?

Sri Krishna explained: Both you and I have passed through many births. I remember them all, but you do not remember. I am birth-less and death-less and Lord of all beings. Yet, due to my divine power – but keeping my power under control, I manifest myself from time to time for protecting the good, for transforming the wicked and for establishing world order (dharma). My birth and activities are divine.

Sri Krishna's Divine Forms

Sri Krishna's forms are countless – varied hues and shapes.

All gods are in His body. Whole universe of the moving and unmoving are all as a unit abide in His body. To see His divine form – the imperishable form, one should have a power of divine vision.

His spiritual forms as the lord of the universe possess many mouths and eyes, many marvellous sights, decked with many divine ornaments, wielding many divine weapons, wearing divine garlands and clothes, anointed with celestial perfumes, with faces on all sides.

If the splendour of a thousand suns were to blaze forth all at once in the sky, that would be like the splendour of Sri Krishna as a Mighty Lord.

Whole universe with its many divisions is drawn together into one. Divine forms have countless arms, stomachs, mouths and eyes on all sides.

Sun and Moon are His Eyes and Burning Fire is His Mouth. His form fills up the space between heaven and earth and quarters. The form has no beginning, middle or end. The divine form is seen with crown, club and chakra;

Sun is like as a mass of radiance blazing everywhere and immeasurable on all sides and heating whole universe. The forms are infinite in power with infinite arms. All venerable praise the divine form with sublime hymns.

On seeing this Divine Forms of Sri Krishna, Arjuna exclaimed: When I see you touching the sky, blazing with many colours, with mouths wide open, with large fiery eyes, my heart trembles in fear and I find neither courage nor peace. I saw all warriors entering into your mouths – terrible with teeth and flaring like the fire at the time of universal destruction.

As many torrents of rivers rush towards the ocean, these heroes in the world flung themselves into your fiercely foaming mouths. As moths rush headlong into a blazing fire for destruction, so do these creatures hurriedly speed into your mouths for their destruction.

Tell me who you are? I also like to know about your purpose, of which I am in ignorance.

Sri Krishna explained: I am the mighty destroyer of the world. Even without you, those warriors arrayed in the enemy's camp must die. These warriors stand already slain by Me. You are only an instrument. Pleased with you I have shown you, through my own power of yoga, this supreme effulgent, primal and infinite cosmic body, which was never seen before by anyone else but you. In this mortal world, I cannot be seen in this form by anyone else but you. Either through study of Vedas or of rituals or again through gifts, actions or austere penances, one cannot see Me in this form which is called Visvaroopa Darshan.

Arjuna's request for Forgiveness:

Arjuna lamented: You are the knower and the knowable and the supreme abode. Salutations to you for your all-pervading form – infinite in might and immeasurable in strength. Pardon Me for addressing you as "O, Krishna, O, Yadava, O, Friend" looking at you merely as a friend ignorant of your greatness. In whatever way I may have insulted you, while at play, sitting or at meals, when alone or in company – for all that I crave forgiveness from You. You are the father of this world moving and unmoving. You are to be adored by this world, you are the greatest guru; none there exists, who is equal to you in the three worlds; who then can excel you, O Being of unequalled power? I implore you to forgive me as a father with a son, as a friend with a friend and as a lover with his beloved. I rejoice that I have seen what was never seen before, but my mind is confounded with fear.

I desire to see You as before in your former form having four arms and crowned with a mace and a discus in the hand. Sri Krishna assumed his gentle form and consoled Arjuna who was terrified.

Sri Krishna's Attributes:

Sri Krishna dwells in all – taste in water, radiance in moon and sun, syllable OM in Vedas, sound in ether, manliness in man, sweet fragrance in earth, brilliance in fire, life in all beings, austerity in ascetics.

Sri Krishna is seated in the hearts of all. He is said to be beyond darkness, knowledge, the knowable, the goal of knowledge. He is the only object worth knowing through Vedas. He is the author of Vedanta as well as the knower of Vedas. He is the beginning, the middle and the end. He is all in this world – sun, moon, senses, consciousness, mountains, ocean, monosyllable OM, Gayathri Mantra, Himalayas, sages Narada and Kapila, Varuna, Yama, time, death, Ganga, fame, fortune, speech, memories, intelligence, constancy and forbearance, splendour, victory, effort, good, silence, wisdom. Of those who debate, He is the reason. There is no being, whether moving or unmoving that can exist without Him. He supports whole universe with a single fragment of Himself.

Sri Krishna is sacrifice, worship, offering, medicinal herb, Vedic hymns, sacrificial fire, father, mother, three Vedas. He is also the supporter, the Lord, the witness, the abode, the shelter, the heat, rain and host of others.

Men versed in Vedas cleansed of their sins by performance of sacrifices drank soma juice. They attained heaven by their meritorious deeds to enjoy heaven. When the asset of meritorious deeds was exhausted, they were born again in the world due to their desires.

Those who worship Sri Krishna are assured of their worldly wants fulfilled and also preservation of their assets. Those who worship other deities and the ghosts go to them. Sri Krishna's worshippers come to Him.

Sri Krishna is undivided whole, yet He seems to be divided due to His dwelling in all beings as if divided into many. He is to be known as the supporter of all beings. He is the destroyer and the creator of all. He has no sense organs, but the faculties of senses function by His power. He is devoid of gunas. He is inside as well as outside all beings. He is unmoving, but He looks like one moving because He is everywhere. He is both far and near – far to the ignorant and near to the knowing. Owing to subtlety, He cannot be known like gross object.

Sri Krishna dwells in the heart of all creatures mounted on vehicles causing them to revolve according to their Karmas by His illusive power called Maya. Body becomes the wheel of the vehicle.

Under Sri Krishna's direction and control, Nature brings out this mighty universe of living and non-living beings. Thus does the wheel of this world revolve. All beings revolve into Nature – He brings all into being and destroys them as well. These activities do not in any way bind Him, because Sri Krishna remains detached like one unconcerned in their midst.

Sri Krishna is the eternal seed of all beings, the intelligence of the intelligent, the splendour of the splendid, the strength of the strong devoid of desire and passion.

Sri Krishna's Supreme Nature:

Sri Krishna is everywhere in this world in His un-manifested being. With hands and feet everywhere, with eyes and heads and mouths everywhere, with ears everywhere – He exists enveloping all.

All objects dwell in Supreme Self or Absolute, but not the Supreme Self in them. Supreme Self is infinite and hence Finite Object only can dwell in Infinite Object. This is similar to the fact that wind (finite) is in space (infinite), but space is not in wind. He is the source and support of all objects and yet not abiding in them.

All beings are same to Sri Krishna and none is hateful and dearer to Him. But those who worship Sri Krishna with devotion dwell in Him and Sri Krishna too dwells in them. A confirmed sinner, on worshiping Him with unwavering faith and devotion, will become a righteous one which begets a lasting peace. No devotee of Sri Krishna will ever perish. Irrespective of caste or creed, all attain to the highest spiritual goal on taking refuge in Sri Krishna.

One who abandons all desires and becomes free from longing and feeling of "I" and "MY" attains peace. There is no time factor to attain the Brahman State. Even at the death hour, a man gets into oneness with Brahman.

In seeing, hearing, touching, smelling, eating, walking, sleeping, breathing, speaking, giving, taking as well as opening and closing of eyes, the wise believes that only the senses are operating upon their objects. And wise man knowing the eternal truth is aware that "I do nothing at all".

Sri Krishna does not create the urge for action, or the feeling of doership, or the attachment to the results of action in people. The powers of material nature do all these. The omnipresent God does not take the responsibility for the good or evil deeds of anybody. As knowledge is enveloped with ignorance, the mortals are constantly falling a prey to delusion about actions.

When the ignorance has been destroyed by the knowledge of God, that knowledge reveals Supreme Being just as the sun reveals the object of the world. Those who think of Supreme always, who are ever at one with Supreme, who are deeply devoted to Supreme, and who look upon Supreme as their goal, get purified of their sins by divine knowledge and go to the state from which there is no return to worldly life.

Any enlightened person is a Brahmin who is endowed with learning and humility. Thus, a Brahmin is one who perceives God in all. Hence such enlightened person looks with equal eye on a cow, an elephant, a dog and an outcaste.

He whose mind is set in equality has accomplished everything in this very life. Such a person has realized Supreme Being, because the Absolute is untouched by evil and knows no distinction. Established in Brahman, with firm understanding and with no delusion, the knower of Brahman rejoices not, getting what is pleasant and grieves not, getting what is unpleasant. With the self-detached to sense objects, through meditation of Brahman, he enjoys the eternal Bliss.

Enjoyments born of sense-objects are indeed the sources of misery and they have a beginning and an end. The wise men do not rejoice in them.

He who is able to withstand the urge arising from passion and anger in this very life, before casting off the body, is a yogi and is a happy man. He whose happiness is within, whose rejoicing is within and whose light is within, that yogi, established in Brahman, attains the beatitude of Brahman. The seers whose sins have been waned away, whose doubts have been dispelled, who have controlled their mind, and who are devoted to the welfare of all beings, attains Supreme Being. Knowing Sri Krishna, the recipient of all sacrifices and asceticism, the supreme lord of all the worlds and the well-wisher of all beings, the devotee attains peace. Seven great sages, Sanakas, Manus were sprung from Sri Krishna's Thought. He is the source of all things – knowing thus the wise worships Sri Krishna with ecstatic devotional fervour. The wise is ever contented and delighted in conversing about Sri Krishna and is enlightened thereby. By dwelling in the hearts of His worshippers, He destroys the ignorance-born darkness by the luminous lamps of wisdom. Sri Krishna is the supreme Brahman, the Supreme Abode and the Supreme Purifier.

The triple designation of Supreme Self is "Om, Tat, Sat."

Om represents Actions.

Tat represents Detachment of Actions

Sat represents Faith of Actions

These actions refer to the sacrifice, gift and austerity.

Whatever is performed as a sacrifice, gift or austerity without faith is declared to be Asat. Asat has no value here or hereafter. Beginningless is the Supreme Brahman. It is neither being (Sat) nor non-being (Asat). If one has really known this truth, he attains to immortality

Yoga of Realization - Maya (illusion):

The three modes of material nature – goodness, passion and ignorance

– also emanate from Sri Krishna. Sri Krishna is not dependent on, or affected by, the modes of material nature; but the modes of material nature are dependent on Sri Krishna. Human beings are deluded by various aspects of these three modes of material nature and they do not know Sri Krishna – the eternal and above these modes. This divine power (Maya) of Sri Krishna consists of three modes of material matter of nature and hence maya is very difficult to overcome. Only those who surrender unto Sri Krishna easily cross over this Maya (illusion).

The evildoers, the ignorant, the lowest persons who are attached to demonic nature, and whose power of discrimination has been taken away by divine illusive power (Maya) do not seek refuge in Sri Krishna. Without any insight into Sri Krishna's transcendental nature, unique and immutable, men of poor understanding look upon Sri Krishna as a mere human individual, having come into manifestation from an un-manifested state.

Sri Krishna is not revealed to all, as He is veiled by Yoga Maya (Divine Illusive Power). Those who take refuge in Sri Krishna and strive for deliverance from old age and death, they realize in full all about the Absolute, His spiritual manifestation and His works of spiritual import. The steadfast persons alone know Sri Krishna as the basic of all – the mortal beings, temporal beings and the Eternal Being. Such steadfast souls, even at the time of death, attain Sri Krishna.

Foolish men do not understand Sri Krishna. His higher nature as Supreme Lord of all that exists also is not known to such foolish men who disregard Him manifested in the human body. Those who are of having the characteristics of demons – viz. cruel, proud and passionate – will never know Sri Krishna. But the ones endowed with virtuous characteristics of celestial forms understand Him as the Immutable and the source of all beings. Such persons always sing His glories and prostrate before Sri Krishna. Others by their wisdom worship Him as one in all and as the inherent in all.

Sri Krishna's Message for Salvation for dying man:

One, who departs from the body, thinking of Sri Krishna at the time of death, attains His state; there is no doubt about it. Thinking of the entity at the time of death by a person decides his fate and cause of his next life journey. Therefore, one should think of Sri Krishna at all times with mind and reason thus set to reach Sri Krishna. If one meditates with devotion even at the time of death with a steady mind and with the power of Yoga properly fixing the life-breath in between the eyebrows on Supreme Self, that person reaches Him.

Concentrate on Sri Krishna as wise, ancient, ruler, smaller than the smallest, inconceivable form, resplendent like the sun and beyond ignorance. And he attains the shining Supreme Self.

Sri Krishna's Message for Time of Death:

The goal into which aspirants bereft of all desires enter is the abode of Imperishable as described in Vedas (Holy Scriptures).

All gates of the body closed, the mind confined within the heart, having fixed his life energy in the head, engaged in firm yoga, uttering the monosyllable – OM, which is Brahman, and thinking of Sri Krishna, he who departs leaving the body, attains the Supreme Goal. Then there is no rebirth.

Time of death also determines salvation and re-birth.

One who dies at the daytime, bright fortnight and six months of the northern course of time – attains to Brahman.

One who dies at night, the black fortnight and the six months of the southern course of the sun – attains the lunar sphere to have re-birth in the world. These two paths of the world, the bright and the dark, are considered to be eternal. Bright path of the departed soul attains birthless state, while the other departed soul in the dark path returns on rebirth to this world. Whoever among Yogis knows these two paths, they are never deluded. Therefore, be steadfast in Yoga at all times. The one who knows all this knowledge goes beyond getting benefits of the study of Vedas, performance of sacrifices, austerities, and charities. That person attains salvation.

Gates of Hell

Three gates of Hell are lust, anger and greed, which are destructive of ~~the~~man's spiritual nature. Therefore, one should abandon these three. If a man is free from these three, he can work out his own good and reach the highest goal. He who abandons the commandments of the scriptures and lives on the impulse of his desires, he attains neither spiritual perfection, nor worldly happiness nor liberation. Therefore, let the scriptures be the authority in determining what should be done and what should not be done. One should perform the duty following the scriptural injunction.

Supreme Abode:

Supreme Abode of Sri Krishna is not illumined by the sun or by the moon or by the fire. Those who are free from pride and delusion, which have conquered the evil of attachment, who are constantly dwelling in Supreme Being with all lust completely stilled, who are free from dualities of pleasure and pain; such wise ones reach His Supreme Abode. Having reached there, people never return to this world.

The eternal Jivatma in this body is a particle of Sri Krishna's own being. The Jiva or Individual Soul attracts the senses with mind as the sixth sense, abiding in the Nature. When the individual soul gets a new body or abandons an old one, the individual soul, the lord of the body, leaves carrying the mind and the senses with him, as the wind carries smells from the blossoming flowers.

Sri Krishna's concluding remarks:

"O, Arjuna! These teachings are never to be spoken by you to one who is devoid of austerities, nor to one who is not devoted, nor to one who does not do service, nor to one who speaks ill of Me. He, who with supreme devotion to Me, will teach this immensely profound philosophy to My devotees, shall doubtless come to Me. ~~alone~~. And he who will study this sacred dialogue of ours, I shall regard it as equivalent of worshipping Me with knowledge sacrifice."

Sanjaya's conviction:

Sanjaya had said this as his final words:

"Thus, I heard this wonderful dialogue between Sri Krishna and Arjuna, causing my hair to stand on end. By the grace of sage Vyasa, I heard this most secret and supreme yoga directly from Sri Krishna, the Lord of Yoga, Himself speaking to Arjuna due to the divine power of my eyes granted by sage Vyasa. Wherever there is Sri Krishna, the Lord of Yoga, accompanied by Arjuna wielding the bow – there reign good fortune, victory, prosperity and sound policy. Such is my conviction."

Section 2: Articles Exploring Sri Krishna

Article 1 - Similes in Bhagavad Gita

Similes add beauty to the slokas. They also clear doubts and create clarity to the subject matter.

In Bhagavad Gita, similes are used in 16 stanzas and the maximum number of similes are used in chapter 2 – five in numbers.

Remaining 11 similes are used one each in stanza pertaining to 7 chapters and 2 similes each in chapters 11 and 18.

Similes used in those 16 stanzas are furnished together with the main object of the similes there against:

Chapter	Stanza	Object of simile
2	22 46 58 67 70	Garments Well water Tortoise Ship Ocean
3	38	Fire-Mirror-Embryo
4	37	Fire
5	10	Lotus
6	19	Lamp

7	7	Beads
11	28 29	Rivers Moths
13	33	Sun
15	8	Wind
18	48 61	Smoke Machine

All similes in the above table are uttered by Sri Krishna except two similes in chapter 11 which are used by Arjuna.

While using the similes of Fire, Beads, Sun, Smoke and Machine, Sri Krishna calls Arjuna by name. By this Lord Krishna perhaps wants to emphasize to Arjuna the importance of the above similes over the others.

On a careful analysis of the objects of the similes, the subject matter for which these similes are used can be brought under the major categories as detailed hereunder:

1. Soul - Garments, Well water, Sun, Wind, Machine.

2. Mind, Intellect and Senses - Tortoise, Ship, Ocean, Fire, Mirror-Embryo, Fire, Lamp, Beads.

3. Duty - Lotus, Smoke

4. Vision - Rivers, Moths

Now, let us know the meaning of the respective stanzas as enunciated in the Gita text.

About Soul:

1. Garments:

Soul discards the old bodies and assumes new bodies. Similarly, human being discards torn garments and wears new garments.

2. Well Water:

When there are plenty of water all around, only a few makes use of well water. In the same way, even the Vedas have only limited use to an enlightened soul.

3. Sun:

O, Bharata! As one sun illumines this whole world, so the Lord of Creation illumines all creations.

4. Wind:

When soul obtains a body and then leaves it, soul takes the mind and the senses from the body. It is similar to the wind carrying the scents from the flowers.

5. Machine:

O, Arjuna! God dwells in the hearts of all beings. God is the cause of all beings to revolve due to His Power of May like objects mounted on a machine.

About Mind, Intellect and Senses:

1.Tortoise:

The intellect of a person is steady, when he withdraws completely his senses from the sense objects just like the tortoise withdraws its limbs into the shell.

2. Ship:

When the mind follows the dictates of the roving senses, that mind is forced to lose its intellect and thereby its directions. The mind is tossed like a ship in the midst of a gale on the high sea.

3. Ocean:

Full ocean is not disturbed by the entry of river waters and will never overflow its shores. Similarly, the person within whose mind all desires dissipate without creating any mental disturbance has attained peace.

Others who desire material objects, are never peaceful.

4. Fire-Mirror-Embryo:

As a Fire is ~~by~~ covered by smoke, a mirror by dust and an embryo by the womb, similarly one's knowledge is covered by the lust.

5. Fire:

O, Arjuna! As the blazing fire reduces wood to ashes, even so, the fire of knowledge reduces all actions to ashes.

6. Lamp:

"As a lamp in a windless place does not flicker" – this is the simile used for the disciplined mind of the yogi practicing meditation on God.

7. Beads:

O, Dhananjaya! There is nothing higher than Me. All in the universe is strung on Me, as a row of beads on a string.

About Duty:

1.Lotus:

Like water remains unattached on lotus leaf, offering all actions to God without attachment remains untouched by sin.

2. Smoke:

O, Son of Kunti! One should not abandon his duty born of one's nature, even if it has defects. Because all duties are tainted with blemish like fire being covered by smoke.

About Vision:

1.Rivers:

Like the swift flowing waters of numerous rivers, the warriors enter Sri Krishna's flaming mouths.

2.Moths:

As the moths rush with great speed into the blazing fire, so worldly creatures enter Krishna's mouths to meet their doom.

Elucidation:

Bhagavad Gita – which literally means "Songs of God" – is really simple in its text and deep in its meaning. Reading and re-reading of the text or its simple translation will make us understand the Gita better.

My attempt is only to make you to 'feel' the Gita in different angle and I scrupulously confine to the bare text of ~~the~~ Gita only.

Article 2 - Analytical Insight into Bhagavad Gita

In my above article no.1, I wrote on the subject of "Similes in Bhagavad Gita".

In the present article, let me examine the various ways by which both Sri Krishna and Arjuna call each other and also about the questions posed by Arjuna to Sri Krishna.

Bhagavad Gita can be considered as questions and answers pertaining to various facets of life as posed by Arjuna and answered by Sri Krishna.

It is my attempt to understand the main text and message of Bhagavad Gita by a very peculiar and different approach so as to focus the various aspects in it and to illumine our journey to get rid of the darkness within and without.

What is in name – some may say and argue, but the names have important place in one's life and they are important to identify one another. It is said that the sweetest word in the world is one's own name and to hear it, when uttered, he becomes most pleased.

An analysis of names used both by Arjuna and Sri Krishna are interesting by themselves.

Arjuna calls Sri Krishna in 17 names 44 times and the details are as under:

Details of Arjuna Callings of Sri Krishna:

S.No.	Nomenclature	Number of Times
1.	Krishna	8 times
2.	Janarthana	6 times
3.	Kesava (Madhusudana)	4 times

4.	Achutha (Purushothama) Deva (Lord of Universal Form)	Both 3 times
5.	Bhagavan Yogi Hrishikesa Prabu Vishnu Govinda Madhava Varshneya	All 2 times
6.	Lotus Eyed Parameswara Mighty Armed Mahatma	All 1 time

It is interesting to note that even in the same stanza, Arjuna uses two names of Sri Krishna, perhaps to draw His attention or rather Arjuna's own dilemma in understanding the eternal truth uttered by Lord Himself.

S. No.	Chapter & Stanza	Sri Krishna's names
1.	Ch. 3 – 1	Janardana Kesava
2.	Ch. 10 – 14	Kesava Bhagavan
3.	Ch. 10 – 17	Yogi Bhagavan
4.	Ch. 11 – 3	Parameswara Purushothama
5.	Ch. 11 – 4	Prabu Yogi
6.	Ch. 11 – 38	Being of Countless Forms Primal God
7.	Ch. 11 – 46	Thousand Armed Universal Form

Arjuna, in some stanzas, uses more than two different names of Sri

Krishna – in ch. 11 – 37 – names used in 6 times and in ch.10 – 15 - names used in 5 times - as detailed below. As these occur in chapter 11 dealing with "The Cosmic Form" and in chapter 10 dealing with "The Divine Glories", Arjuna's ecstasies are to be attributed to his calling Sri Krishna in many names as if in complete trance with intense prayer mood.

The details are as under:

1.	Ch. 11 – 37	Mahatma Imperishable God of Gods Universe Brahma Infinite
2.	Ch. 10 – 15	Purushothama Creator Lord of Beings God of Gods Ruler of the World
3.	Ch. 11 – 45	Deva God of Gods Universe
4.	Ch. 18 – 1	Hrishikesa Mighty Armed Slayer of Kesi

Let us analyse how Sri Krishna calls Arjuna who, casting aside his bow and arrow, sat on the chariot with his mind overwhelmed with sorrow and who had declared in an unambiguous tone – "I will not fight".

Sri Krishna calls Arjuna by 17 names 141 times and the details are as under:

S. No.	Nomenclature	No. of times
1.	Partha	32 times
2.	Bharatha	24 times
3.	Son of Kunti	23 times
4.	Arjuna	22 times
5.	Mighty Armed	12 times
6.	Dhananjaya	7 times
7.	Scorcher of foes	6 times
8.	Best of Men Kuru Dynasty Pandava	5 times
9.	Scion of Bharata Race	4 times
10.	Sinless One	3 times
11.	Awakened One	2 times
12.	Son Best of the embodied Tiger Savyasachin (Capable of shooting arrows even by left hand)	1 time

Sri Krishna is using two names of Arjuna in the same stanza the details of which are furnished hereunder. Of course, it is observed that there is no stanza with more than two names of Arjuna, while Arjuna uses more names in addressing Sri Krishna as analysed above.

Details are as under:

S. No.	Reference Chapter	Nomenclature
1.	Ch. 4 – 5	Arjuna Scorcher of Foes
2.	Ch. 4 – 33	Scorcher of Foes

		Bharatha
3.	Ch. 6 – 35	Mighty Armed Son of Kunti
4.	Ch. 6 – 40	Partha Son
5.	Ch. 8 – 27	Partha Arjuna
6.	Ch. 11 – 54	Scorcher of Foes Arjuna
7.	Ch. 18 – 34	Partha Arjuna
8.	Ch. 18 – 72	Partha Dhananjaya

The following factors emerge, while categorizing the names mentioned above in the order of number of times:

S. No.	Nomenclature	No. of times
1.	Arjuna	4 times
2.	Partha	4 times
3.	Scorcher of Foes	3 times
4.	Bharatha Mighty Armed Son of Kunti Son Dhananjaya	1 time

To conclude, one interesting factor emerges:

Arjuna calls Sri Krishna by 17 different names repeated only 44 times at different stanzas, whereas, Sri Krishna uses 17 different names of Arjuna, He repeats them as many as 141 times.

Why should Sri Krishna call Arjuna by so many times and in so many places? – One may ponder.

The answer is not far to seek.

Arjuna is in an utter state of confusion and with grief engulfed and he refuses 'to act' and his refusal is in the midst of battlefield.

It has fallen on the shoulders of Sri Krishna to make Arjuna to realize his faults and to make Arjuna to take up arms. It is rightly said that the sweetest of all word is one's own name and Sri Krishna, perhaps, wants to please Arjuna's ears with his own name a number of times which will be more effective means of convincing him rather than reasoning though Sri Krishna has almost exhausted all his powers of arguments ~~as gospel~~ in Bhagavad Gita.

Sri Krishna calls Arjuna as 'Son' once in ch.6 – 40 which clearly indicates that Arjuna is bound to follow his advice – as the son's duty is to simply obey father's advice even without waiting for reasons there for. But, as a Supreme Father, Sri Krishna has, however, explained in detail to Arjuna all the facts so as to allow him to take his own decision – without imposing the decision on Arjuna.

Decision taken on conviction and not on compulsion will ensure complete dedication in accomplishing the tasks ahead.

One more revealing observation is that Sri Krishna uses Partha for 32 times which top the list followed by Bharatha – 24 times, leaving Arjuna far below at 22 times.

Perhaps, Sri Krishna's favourite name of Arjuna is Partha and not Arjuna, as far as Bhagavad Gita is concerned.

Article 3 - Arjuna's Questions to Sri Krishna

Bhagavad Gita can be considered as philosophical and spiritual discussions between Arjuna and Sri Krishna about the ultimate truth and the ways and means to attain the same.

Bhagavad Gita contains 18 chapters and 700 verses. Of these 574 were delivered by Sri Krishna, 84 by Arjuna, and 41 by Sanjaya. One verse — the first one was by Dhritarashtra.

And 142 verses in five chapters (chapters – 7, 9, 13, 15 and 16) are Sri Krishna's own words and not in answers to Arjuna's specific questions. These deal mainly with Lord Himself. In these chapters, Arjuna had not spoken a word.

The details of chapters are furnished hereunder:

Chapter 7 - Yoga of Knowledge and Realisation – Total Verses:30

Chapter 9 - Yoga of Sovereign Science and Sovereign Secret – **Total Verses:34**

Chapter 13 - Yoga of the Discrimination between Nature and Soul – **Total Verses:34**

Chapter 15 - Yoga of the Supreme Self – Total Verses:20

Chapter 16 - Yoga of Division between the divine and the demoniacal – Total Verses:24

These details are given only to understand Bhagavad Gita in the proper-perspective and also to help those who are interested to know the specific answers of Sri Krishna to Arjuna's questions.

Arjuna had placed 16 questions before Sri Krishna on various subjects such as knowledge, action, devotion, mind and God.

Before going to the text of the questions of Arjuna, the details below will throw some insights into the aspects under which Arjuna wanted answers and clarifications:

S. No.	Main Topic	Specific Subjects on which Arjuna seeks Sri Krishna's answers
1.	Yoga of Knowledge	1. Body 2. Soul 3. Sin 4. Which is superior – knowledge or action?
2.	Yoga of Action	1 Renunciation (sanyasa). 2. Relinquishment or yoga of selfless services (action abandoning its fruits - i. e. action without attachment or simply tyaga) 3. Which of these – renunciation or relinquishment – is the best?
3.	Yoga of Devotion	1. Who is dear to Sri Krishna? 2. Methods of worship – Form and Formless 3. Worship with faith – not as per scriptures.
4.	Mind	1. Steady Wisdom 2. Sin due to Lust 3. Meditations or Control of Senses 4. Three Modes of Material Nature or Three Gunas –Sattva, Rajas, Tamas representing three qualities of nature viz human goodness, human passion and human ignorance.
5.	God	1. Form 2. Nature 3. Powers and Glories

Now let us plunge into the actual questions of Arjuna posed to Sri Krishna in all humility as an obedient disciple in complete surrender with full faith and absolute reverence as a student towards his teacher.

The sixteen questions are listed below in the same order in which the questions were asked along with the details of the verses for easy identification.

Understanding the questions themselves are the first step to fathom the secret wealth of Bhagavad Gita.

Question No.1: What is the duty that is good?

Chapter 2 – Verse No.7: My natural disposition is vitiated by a sense of pity, and my mind is in utter confusion regarding my duty. Tell me that which is definitely good for me. I am your disciple; I have taken refuge in you; teach me.

Question No.2: What is the definition of steady wisdom?

Chapter 2 – Verse No.54: What is the definition, O Kesava, of a man of steady wisdom, absorbed in contemplation? How does a man of steady wisdom talk, sit and walk?

Question No.3: Distinction between knowledge and action – which one will give bliss?

Chapter 3 – Verses Nos. 1 & 2: If in your opinion, O Janardana, knowledge is superior to action, then, why do you, O Kesava, urge me to engage in this terrific war? Due to these apparently conflicting advices, I am confused; tell me only that leads to my highest good.

Question No.4: What is the compelling force by which the man commits sin?

Chapter 3 – Verse No.36: What is that, O Varshneya, prompted by which a man is forced to live a sinful life even against his will?

Question No.5: Simple clarification about Sri Krishna's

Incarnation.

Chapter 4 – Verse No.4: You are of recent origin, while the birth of Vivaswan (sun god) date back to remote antiquity. How, then, am I to believe that you taught this Yoga at the beginning of creation?

Question No.6: Performance of Action and Renunciation of Action – which is good?

Chapter 5 – Verse No.1: O Krishna, you praise both renunciation of actions and performance of actions. Now, tell me with certainty which is of them leads to one's good.

Question No.7: What are the ways to control the restless mind to attain permanent equanimity?

Chapter 6 – Verse Nos. 33 – 34: O Slayer of Madhu, you have said that the yoga of meditation is characterised by the equanimity of mind, but I do not see any permanence, owning to restlessness of the mind.

O Krishna, the mind is restless, turbulent, strong and obstinate. To Control it, I think, is as difficult as controlling the wind.

Question No.8: What is the fate of those who, though having faith in yoga of meditation, has failed due to restlessness of mind?

Chapter 6 – Verses Nos. 37 – 39: What, O Krishna, is the fate of a man who, though endowed with a firm faith, is not steadfast in his practices owing to distractions, and therefore fails to reach spiritual perfection?

O Mighty Armed Lord, strayed from the path leading to God-Realization and without anything to stand upon, is he not lost like the torn cloud, deprived of both God-Realization and heavenly enjoyment?

This doubt of mine, O Krishna, you should dispel in its entirety, for there is none else but you who can remove this doubt.

Question No.9: Questions are being asked to know the Absolute, the

Spirit, Action, Matter, Divinities and further, how to realise the Supreme Being at the time of death by persons of steadfast minds?

Chapter 8 – Verses Nos. 1 – 2: What is Absolute (Brahman)? What is the Spirit (Adhyatma)? What is action (Karma)? What is called Matter (Adhibhuta)? What is termed as Divinities (Adhidaiva)?

O slayer of Madhu, who is the Supreme Being and how does He dwell in the body? How does a man of steadfast mind meditate on the Supreme Being at the time of death?

Question No.10: Methods for meditation.

Chapter 10 – Verses Nos. 17 – 18: O Master of Yoga, through what process of continuous meditation shall I know you? And in what particular forms are You to be meditated upon by me?

O Janardana, tell me once more in detail about Your powers and glories; because listening to your nectar-like words does not satiate me.

Question No.11: Arjuna's desire to see the Cosmic Form of Sri Krishna

Chapter 11: Verses Nos. 1 – 4: Thanks to the most profound words of spiritual wisdom that You have spoken out of kindness to me, this delusion of mine has entirely disappeared.

O Lotus Eyed One! I have heard from You in detail an account of the evolution and dissolution of beings, and also Your Immortal Glory.

Lord, you are precisely what You declare yourself to be. But I long to see Your divine form – possessed of wisdom, glory, energy, strength, valour and effulgence, O Best of Persons!

Krishna, if You think that I can see your cosmic form, then, O Lord of Yoga, reveal to me your imperishable form.

Question No.12: Arjuna requests Sri Krishna to tell about the Primal Being and His Purpose

Chapter 11: Verses Nos.11 – 31: Tell me who You are with a form so terrible? My obeisance to you, O best of gods, be kind to me. I wish to know You, the Primal Being, in particular; for I know not Your purpose.

Question No.13: Worship of Form and Formless – which is the best?

Chapter 12: The ever-steadfast devotees worshiping the personal aspect of God with form and others worshiping the impersonal aspect or the formless Absolute – which of these has the best knowledge of yoga?

Question No.14: Three modes of material nature – Three Gunas – Sattva, Rajas, Tamas

Chapter 14: Verse No.21: What are the marks of the being conquering the three Gunas and what his conduct? And how, Lord, does he rise above the three Gunas?

Question No.15: Status of worshipers with faith, but not as per scriptures.

Chapter 17: Verse No.1: There are persons offering worship full of faith, but without observing scriptural injunctions while doing so – of what nature is their Faith? Is it born of Sattva, Rajas or Tamas?

Question No.16: Distinction between Renunciation and Relinquishment

Chapter 18: Verse No.1: O Hrishikesa, O mighty armed One, O Slayer of Keshin! I desire to know the true nature of renunciation (Sanyasa) and relinquishment (Tyaga).

Conclusion:

Sri Krishna answers all the questions put forth by Arjuna in detail giving no room for any further doubts. It is necessary to know and understand Sri Krishna Himself as illustrated in Bhagavad Gita.

There are three sources in Bhagavad Gita by which we can know Sri Krishna.

1. Foremost is Sri Krishna Himself who speaks about Himself.
2. The second one is Arjuna who describes Sri Krishna on seeing the Cosmic Form of Sri Krishna.
3. The third one is that of Sanjaya – the charioteer of King Dhritarashtra – the blind and father of Duryodhana, who describes in detail about the power and glories of Sri Krishna on seeing Sri Krishna's Cosmic Form.

Article 4 – Who is dear to Sri Krishna?

Sri Bhagavan Krishna declares in chapter 12 – stanzas 13 to 20 (7 in numbers) (Refer page 35) that devotees are dear to him. But Sri Krishna seems to contradict His own statement of this in his declarations in chapter 9 – stanza 29 when he says: "I am the same to all beings; to Me there is none hateful, none dear."

Let us analyse the seemingly contradictory statements of Sri Krishna.

Swami Tapasyananda of Sri Ramakrishna Math, Mylapore has this to explain "The meaning of stanza 29 of chapter 9 can be interpreted as: For Sri Krishna, all are alike and to Him, none is hostile. If you find a difference in His relationship with devotees, it is only because the devotees cling to Him, and so He to them also. However degenerate a man may be, he is free to devote himself to His worship."

Is God then partial towards His devotees as against those who do not adore Him?

Those who adore Him approach close to Him and dwell in Him, and therefore participate in His blissful nature, whereas the others ignorantly or deliberately exclude themselves from Him and become exclusively interested in worldly life with its inevitable consequences.

God is Kalpataru – the wish-yielding tree of heaven. Those who go under the tree and pray are rewarded. Those who exclude themselves from it fail to get those blessings due to their own fault.

A question may now arise: "Is God then simply a passive element like beauties of Nature? Is He not responsive to the devotee's attitude? Does not the devotee get any active help from Him?"

Sri Ramakrishna answers this declaring that if the devotee takes two steps towards Him, He takes ten steps to the devotee. A devotee will find from experience that God's grace works on him in a hundred ways without his actually knowing it.

The last seven stanzas in chapter 12 give graphic details of the devotees who are dear to Sri Krishna. Those who are ego-less, self-controlled, free from joy, anger, fear and anxiety, treating foe and friend alike as explained in the stanzas are dear to Sri Krishna.

Sri Krishna's attitudes are not discriminatory with the human beings – both with his devotees and non-devotees. But the devotees are really near to Sri Krishna as compared with His non-devotees. The swell of his blessings will be more effective on the devotees rather than others – in view of the nearness of His devotees. The benefit of His Grace will be more on the devotees rather than others, though Sri Krishna has no distinctions between the two.

Sun rays falls on the mirror, water and sand. The reflective power of the rays depends upon the surface on which the sun's rays fall.

In mirror, it is the most effective as compared with water and the least in respect of sand.

Devotees are like mirror and water, whereas non-devotees are like sand.

Hence the seemingly contradictory statements are only complimentary in contents.

Article 5 - Man of Steadfast Wisdom

Sri Bhagavan Krishna explains about Man of Steadfast Wisdom in detail in chapter 2 – slokas 55 to 72 (Refer page 43). His explanations run to 18 slokas in chapter 2 – Yoga of Knowledge. As man of steadfast wisdom is described in yoga of knowledge, Sri Krishna indicates that such a man's character is to acquire absolute and eternal knowledge through Gnana Yoga.

In sloka 54 of chapter 2 of Gnana Yoga, Arjuna poses this question to know about Gnani: "O, Kesava ! What are the characteristics of man of steady wisdom with divine consciousness? How does he speak? How does he sit? How does he walk?"

Questions asked by Arjuna about man of steady wisdom are very distinct and specific, but answers are not straight in clear terms for easy understanding. Actually, Sri Krishna's elucidations to Arjuna's specific questions about man of steadfast wisdom – Gnana Yogi are shrouded with symbolism which needs to be deciphered with utmost care and diligent as otherwise it will land us in confusion and doubts.

Arjuna wants to know about three specific activities of Gnana Yogi – viz speech, sitting and walking. But, for these three aspects of his questions, there are no direct answers from Sri Krishna.

To know what Sri Krishna has in his mind to describe about man of steadfast wisdom in respect of his specific activity, it would be ideal to treat these three specific questions as one in general terms – viz. "How does man of steadfast wisdom behave in life generally?"

Gist of the characteristics of man of steadfast wisdom is here below:

- His Mind will be unperturbed by forces of sense objects.
- He controls his mind through meditation.
- He overcomes ego thereby attains peace with the realization of God which is the ultimate goal of a soul.

1. How man of steadfast wisdom speaks:

Man of steadfast wisdom will speak about – how best one can control his senses, what is the real wisdom, how to be free from ego, how to get peace of mind, how to attain brahman state which is the ultimate goal of all embodied soul. In short, man of steadfast wisdom will 'speak' through his own practice of Gnana Yoga.

(Thrust in Sri Krishna's answer: Speech needs to reflect the purity of mind and sublime nature of senses thereby ensuring peace of mind to the listeners.)

2. How man of steadfast wisdom sits:

A disciplined person, enjoying sense objects with senses under control and free from attachments and aversions, attain tranquillity. Tranquillity destroys all sorrows. The intellect of such a tranquil person becomes completely steady and united with the Supreme. He becomes a man of steadfast wisdom.

He sits in Meditation after bringing the senses under control and fixing the mind firmly on God. For he, whose senses are mastered, is known to have a stable mind.

(Thrust in Sri Krishna's answer is: Gnani needs to sit quite often in meditation to attain tranquillity of mind)

3. How man of steadfast wisdom walks:

Soul, which sleeps without realizing the supreme bliss, that time is day to the seer. The ever- changing transient happiness, which keeps awake the being, that time is night to the seer. One attains peace within whose mind all desires dissipate without creating any mental disturbance, as river waters enter the full ocean without creating any disturbance.

(Thrust in Krishna's answer: Figuratively speaking, the man of steadfast mind walks during the real 'day' and enters peacefully the Brahman State).

The practical aspects pertaining to man of wisdom need our attention as well:

Speech: His erudition displayed in delivering speech or discourse about intellectual, religious and spiritual matter pertaining to Vedas.

1. **Sitting:** His siting posture reminiscent of meditative mood.
2. **Walking:** His walk with his disciples to refresh body and mind.

Article 6 - Maya

Specific Mentions of Maya are found in chapter 7 – slokas 14 and 25 and chapter 18 – sloka 61 of Bhagavad Gita.

While chapter 7 with 30 slokas deals with realization of Divine Knowledge, chapter 18 containing maximum number of 78 slokas in Bhagavad Gita deals with Renunciation.

Slokas' meanings are hereunder:

❖ Maya is my divine energy made up of three gunas. Hence Maya is hard to overcome. Still, those who take refuge in Sri Krishna cross over Maya. (ch 7 - sloka 14)

❖ Yoga Maya is a veil of Sri Krishna. Hence Sri Krishna is not revealed to all human beings due to this Mystic and Divine Yoga Maya. Sri Krishna being Unborn and Unchangeable, the deluded world does not know Him. ch. 7 - sloka 25)

❖ Sri Krishna dwells in the hearts of all beings. Maya causes all beings to revolve, as though mounted on a machine. (ch.18 - sloka 61)

Maya like Yoga is a difficult subject to completely understand its various implications and aspects.

In the above slokas, Maya is defined as under:

1. Maya is Sri Krishna's Divine and Mystic Energy made up of Three Gunas.
2. Maya is Sri Krishna's veil which prevents embodied souls to have his darshan and ultimately liberation.
3. Maya can be got rid of with complete surrender to Sri Krishna.

To my knowledge, Maya has two facets – viz 1. Religious and Spiritual and 2. Philosophical and Rational.

Maya may be God's Energy for religious/spiritual aspects but it is Illusion for rational mind. But both schools of thoughts agree that Maya which is a veil over God or Object, needs to be removed to have the real picture of God or Object.

Though Maya is normally attributed to Illusion, Sri Krishna declares it as His Divine Energy.

Human beings propelled by three gunas find it very difficult to overcome Maya to reach the lotus feet of Sri Krishna who is Unborn and Unchanging. Though Sri Krishna is omnipotence, omnipresence and omniscience but Yoga Maya like a curtain hides these attributes. But, Sri Krishna declares, with complete surrender to Him with practice of yogas, Maya's effects will vanish. Then in the absence of Maya's effects, Sri Krishna is revealed.

'Surrender to Me to overcome the influences of Maya and Be blessed to see Me in my divine form – Visvaroopa Darshan' – are His Sermon to overpower Maya.

The word "Maya" is made from Ma (not) and Ya (what is). Thus, Maya means "that which is not what it appears to be." Shri P. D. Shastri, an exponent of Gita, states that meaning of Maya is "appearance, not mere illusion". Perhaps it can be taken to mean – Illusory Appearance.

Role of Maya is to serve God to drive away non-eligible human souls to have darshan of Sri Krishna. Maya by refusing entries to such impure human souls to reach God indirectly enjoins upon them to practice - Yogas of Karma, Gnana and Bhakthi – all or any one of them - overpowering three gunas and thereby make themselves eligible for entries to the abode of Sri Krishna. Maya is thus a gatekeeper to God's

Abode.

1. Religious and Spiritual Aspects of Maya:

Maya is responsible for creating hurdles to understand Brahmin. Maya is illusion of Brahman which will vanish with the dawn of knowledge. Vedic Knowledge can help human beings to take the cloak or veil of Maya hiding Brahman thereby paving ways to liberations.

Various Hindu Scriptures explain characteristics of Maya.

1. Yoga Vasistha's Explanations of Maya: "When the dirt is removed from the particle, it is visible clearly. Similarly, when the darkness is dispelled, objects shrouded by the darkness are visible clearly. When Maya which is Ignorance like darkness, is dispelled, Brahman is realised.

2. Svetasvatara Upanishad declares Brahman – as Mayin – Mayavi who created the world. At that time, Brahman created Maya resembling Himself. It also describes Maya as a magician.

3. Vishnu Purana states that Maya is both formless and form.

4. Rig Veda describes Maya as magic, illusion and power. Further, it adds that Maya is of two kinds – Divine Maya and Undivine Maya, Divine Maya representing truth and Undivine Maya representing untruth.

5. Atharvana Veda states that Maya means power of creation – not illusion.

In short, Maya is main hurdle for embodied souls to get liberation and it is most powerful entity to overcome.

One could then ask, "Is it impossible to overcome Maya?"

Sri Krishna says, "Those who surrender themselves to Me as the Supreme God, then by My grace, they will smoothly cross the ocean of material existence. Then, I will instruct Maya to leave this soul, as it has become Mine now."

On Sri Bhagavan Krishna's instructions, Maya - the material energy of God -simply releases the surrendered soul from its clutches. It says, "My job is to keep troubling the soul until it surrenders at the feet of Sri Krishna; once the soul reaches there, my job is complete."

Now let us know more about Maya as per religious text.

Yoga Maya was the daughter of Nanda and Yashoda. Yoga Maya was also Sri Krishna's sister. Sri Krishna was the eighth child of Devaki and Vasudeva and Yoga Maya was born at the same time at the house of Nanda and Yashoda. As instructed by Almighty, Vasudeva replaced Sri Krishna with daughter of Yashoda. When Kamsa tried to kill this child, the child escaped from his clutches and appeared as Goddess Durga with eight arms with weapons. The Divine Devi told Kamsa that she was Yoga Maya and that his killer was born and that he was sure to be killed.

In Vaishnava sect, Maya – an incarnation of Goddess Durga is called Narayani – Vishnu's powers of illusion.

Hence Maya, whatever may be the views held by philosophers and rationalists, is given a godly status and is worshipped by Hindus.

There are two temples for Yoga Maya – one at Vindhyachal – Mirzapur on the banks of Ganges in UP. Another shrine is located in Bandla, Himachal Pradesh, also called Bandla Mata Temple.

2.Philosophical and Rational Aspects of Maya:

Every entity has two aspects – a hidden inner core i.e., its true nature and a false appearance. This co-existence of true nature and appearance in entities is called Maya.

Appearance alone is accepted as true at first. But the reality dawns on man far late due to the prevalence of ignorance and the absence of knowledge.

False appearance in the entity is purely due to ignorance, which can vanish with the occurrence of knowledge.

The nature of Maya can well be explained by the following examples:

1. A man treads on a rope in the street while walking in darkness and he is frightened mistaking the rope to a snake. Due to darkness, which is akin to ignorance, true nature of the rope has been identified with a false appearance of snake. Light, which is akin to knowledge, clears the false appearance of snake and makes the man to realize true nature of the object i.e., a rope.
2. Cloud is created due to sunrays. After its creation, it hides sun light for a while. Similarly, Yoga Maya hides the greatness of Supreme God for a while. The beings should not be deluded by such Yoga Maya, which never affect Supreme Being.
3. Straight stick seems to be bending, when it is immersed in water. It is illusion or Maya and when the stick is taken out of the water, it regains its original shape.

Such Maya can be overcome by practice of meditation. Sun rays, when passing through lenses, burn the article on which it is focused. In the same way, when mind is focused by meditation, power or energy is tremendous. Veil of Yoga Maya can thus be burnt to win over.

Maya is taken by some as non-existence or illusion. But Maya is not illusion; it is misconception of the real. The real always exists. It is always misread by our senses. So, Maya has no reality, it has only an appearance, but of something contrary to reality. It also hides reality.

Maya is terribly effective in our ignorance. So, it is there. Yet in the end it is not. It exists; it exists not. Yes, Maya is a mystery. Such is the characteristics of Maya.

Maya is also eluding man to understand the real self-i.e., Atma.

Three states of man which he daily passes through viz. waking, dream and deep sleep can explain and prove the existence of Atma which is the real witness of all our actions – with body, mind and ego.

When awake, man identifies himself with body, mind and ego. While asleep with dreams, man dissociates himself with body, but he now identifies with mind and ego – as he thinks that he does many things and enjoys. When he is in deep sleep without any dreams, body, mind and ego also cease functioning. Man says, "I knew nothing, but I slept comfortably." Hence there is **"something"** which enjoys comfort even without help from body with sense organs, mind and ego, which were the source of joy till now. So, sleep proves that "something" which cognizes the functioning of ego, mind and body and their absence as well, can exist without any of these. This "something" is the Atma. This real position is veiled due to Maya.

When man says that he is tall or he is fat, he is fair or dark, man actually identifies himself with body and not with Atma. Similarly, when he says that he is blind or deaf, he identifies himself with sense organs. Again, he identifies himself with mind, when he says that he is confused, he is clear. Thus man, initially and for life suffers from obstinate, false identifications which is termed as Maya.

Then, what is the solution to overcome Maya?

There are three instruments of knowledge to help human being to overcome Maya.

They are:

1.Cognition by senses.

2. Knowledge by reason.

3. Scriptures.

In Sanskrit, these are termed as Pratyaksha, Anumana and Sastra respectively. But man in spite of these tools for acquiring knowledge still lacks real knowledge about Atma. Understanding fully about Atma alone is capable of conquering Maya.

When realization of Atma – famous utterances in Chandogya Upanishad – "Thou Art That" - is achieved, then man is amidst Bliss which will completely overpower the Maya.

But Sri Krishna's prescriptions to conquer this Maya are very straight and simple.

Sri Bhagavan Krishna says:

"The divine Maya of Mine is hard to surmount. I am not revealed to all, as I am veiled by yoga Maya. I dwell in the hearts of all beings, but due to my Maya, all beings revolve as though mounted on a machine. But those who take refuge in Me alone, they cross over this Maya."

MAYA – ILLUSIVE AND ELUSIVE:

The explanations of Sri Krishna of Maya as mentioned above need some critical examinations to comprehend the influences and effects of Maya – the most elusive and confusing and conflicting Force of Almighty on the human beings struggling to overcome this Maya to know True Self in and out.

Sri Krishna uses a simile of – Yantra or Machine or Wheel – in the context of explaining His Maya Power.

Slokas in ch 3 – 16 and ch 18 – 61 contain the simile of Machine.

The textual meanings of these two slokas are hereunder:

Free Style Translation of slokas:

Sloka ch 3 – 16:O Partha ! One needs to learn while living on earth the Revolving Machine or Wheel under the control of Maya. Learning from revolving wheel means to avoid sinful life and uncontrollable joys from senses. Such human souls live meaningful life devoid of vanity.

Sloka ch 18 – 61: O Arjuna, God resides in the heart of all creatures. God causes them to revolve according to their karma by God's Maya – God's Illusive Power. This resolution happens because the human being is mounted on wheels being propelled by Maya.

Preceding and succeeding slokas to 16 and 61 declare that sacrifice as prescribed by Vedas performed by humans results in realisation of God is the solution to overcome Maya. Complete and unconditional surrender of human souls to Almighty will help to win over Maya by which human beings are blessed with the darshan of Almighty in All His splendours.

With these inputs, let us try to unravel the mystery of Maya and its power to lift his veil to get the glimpse of Shri Bhagavan Krishna by humans.

Maya as perceived by human soul is influenced by three gunas – Sattva, Rajas and Tamas. Three gunas in turn are influenced by five elements of nature.

Control of five elements of nature – fire (eyes – 4%), nose (earth – 12%), mouth (water – 72%), ears (ether -6%) and body (air – 6%) - is made difficult due to actions of seeing, smelling, tasting, hearing and touching of worldly objects by human beings whose minds and intellects failing them miserably to be their friends, philosophers and guides. Every sense organ of human beings – being uncontrollable by both mind and intellect - ego joining them to fuel further their ill effects thereby making the veil of Maya thicker and thicker and stronger and stronger and longer and longer. Because of these, the path to reach abode of Almighty is strewn with multiple stones of hurdles - evil eyes, non-meditative nose, gluttony mouth, unholy ears and sensuous body.

Spiritual knowledge and practice have the power to un-screen Maya's veil thereby paving our way to travel towards Supreme God.

Hence if we surrender completely to Sri Bhagavan Krishna with our body, mind and ego, then we have won the battle against Maya – the most eluding factor in the realization of the Real from the Unreal.

Article 7 - Good Action, Bad Action and No Action

You are traveling in a train. The trees seen through the windows of the train are moving fast depending upon the speed of the train. The train and yourself in the train are moving, but the trees are fixed to the ground and are static without any movement. But, your movement - i.e., action of yours is being imposed on the static trees, which makes them to appear as if moving. This is called 'inaction in action' – inaction of tree affected by action of man. Action of your movement is imposed on inactive trees.

In the sea, a ship, which is moving, seems to be motionless for the man at the shore. Similarly, moon is moving, but to you, it seems to be motionless. The movement of ship and moon ends up in inaction for the man in the shore who has no action. Here action is 'action in inaction'. That is action of ship/moon is imposed on the inactive man.

Earth is revolving, but its action of revolving is not felt by us. This is also called action in inaction.

Let us think about the spinning top in action. Top is rotating very fast and, in that state, it appears to be static, motionless or action-less. This is a classic example of action in inaction.

Let us recall one more aspect of action and inaction.

Physical action of body and mental action of mind are not always in tune with each other. One might have finished his work – physical body's action, but his mind will not cease to think about the completed action of his. In that state, such person may appear to be inactive having completed his work; but, if his mind is pondering over his past action, he will be considered as active – if not physical but mental. It is called 'inaction in action'- inactive physically – active mentally.

What is the purpose of narrating the phenomenon of 'action in inaction' and 'inaction in action'?

The above narrations are only prelude to explain the intricate meanings of one of the important stanzas in Bhagavad Gita in chapter 4 – stanza 18.

The translated version of the stanza is: **He who sees inaction in action and action in inaction is enlightened among men. He is a yogi. He has completed all actions.**

Here Good or Beneficial Action is called Karma. Bad or Baneful Action is Vikarma. No Action is called Akarma.

'Akarma in Karma' i.e. inaction in action and 'Karma in Akarma' i.e. action in inaction need some critical examinations.

Characteristic of soul or atma is no action. No action does not mean inactivity. Body and mind are carrying out actions and soul is witness – as non-attached self. Those who do actions non-attached to fruits of actions and fully satisfied and free from expectations are deemed to have done nothing, even though engaged in action. No sin is attached to such action. This state is called 'Akarma' or no action.

Idleness should not be confused with akarma or no action. Idle person keeps willfully idle and says he had abandoned action and was restful. Here he is only identifying himself with body-mind without any perception of soul – consciousness. His physical workless-ness, whether forcefully adopted or born of idleness, is not to be treated as no action. Inaction is not idleness – it is actually surcharged with energy.

One aspect of akarma is that, though man acts, he does not act. Other aspect is that, though he does not act at all, he moves whole world to action. There is in him an immeasurable power to impel to action. This is the paradox of akarma. It is filled with a power that is capable of infinite action. It is like steam which when compressed, does enormous work.

A child does a mistake and its father and mother stop speaking to it. It will create a terrible effect on the child. Not speaking is far more effective than any kind of physical hands of action.

Silence can achieve what speaking cannot. This non-action, silence, sitting still, accomplishes much, releases great power of action. What action cannot achieve, some person, remaining inactive, accomplishes. The presence of some leaders will ensure control and discipline in the crowd, even though they will be silent. Their power of presence is enough to ensure the desired effect and hence they are actually in the mode of 'no action'.

Actions have both ethical and metaphysical ramifications. Right or moral action and wrong or immoral action falls in the sphere of ethics. What distinguishes action from inaction is a metaphysical question

Ethical aspect of action is difficult to define. If we seek the guidance of religions for ethics, right conduct as prescribed by the scriptures is at variance amongst themselves. Thus, what is right action and what is wrong action cannot be known or defined with firmness and certainty due to different interpretations given in different religious texts.

Rationalism also fails to define ethics effectively without giving room for confusion. Theory of rationalism equating ethics of action based on the greatest good of the greatest number is not agreed or approved by all and there is no consensus to support this theory.

Metaphysical aspect of action is still more difficult to evaluate. What is real action and what is true inaction are difficult to determine. Inaction comes to fruition, when the man mixes his action with knowledge of dedication and detachment. This can be explained by an example. One man cooks regularly and this becomes his action. When he becomes expert in his cooking, his action becomes inaction in the sense that the man does his action effortlessly and efficiently and he becomes knowledgeable in his action of cooking. With attainment of this state of efficiency, the cook will cook effortlessly – as if he is not cooking at all. This is called action in inaction i.e., attainment of complete knowledge in action.

Adi Sankarara's interruptions of actions are worth recalling. According to Adi Sankara, actions are undertaken to ward off evil and attain good. A cow will be attracted towards a man with a grass and will run away from a man with a stick. These are due to its instinct nature. Similarly, even man's resorting to action to attain good and ward off evil is natural to him by his instinct. Man, resorts to Karma attracted by its good results, as the cow resorts to grass. He resorts to it not because of Veda's call to him but because of the urge of his desire.

Sankara's implications are that non-performance of Karma will not entail evil consequences; no command has been disobeyed here, as there was no command. Sankara affirms that Vedas are not the commands of God and so are not mandatory. He further confirms that Vedas reveal truths and do not issue any commands.

There are dolls of animals and birds made of gold. If a child sees the dolls, the forms of the dolls will attract and the child will not be interested in the substance i.e., gold. But a goldsmith will be interested in the substance i.e., gold rather than the forms.

The goldsmith will only look at the weight of the gold and not its form in evaluating it. The form is relevant to him only in so far as it reveals the substance, which is his sole concern. Through all forms, the goldsmith sees only the substance. So, through all actions and objects, the enlightened one sees the substance, the God or Almighty.

Let me end up this article with the quote from Gandhiji:

"Karma becomes relatively akarma when it is undertaken for the service of others, for the sake of our higher good. We may be said to eat and breathe with that aim only if we have voluntarily and deliberately dedicated our body to the service of Shri Krishna. He who lives with the knowledge that his body is not his, that God makes it dance as He wills, may be said to have realized God. All karma does in that spirit is akarma. Anything else, though seemingly akarma, is in truth karma."

Article 8 - Yoga, Sanyasa and Tyaga

Reader is fond of reading Bhagavad Gita. He is now faced with doubts as to the real meaning of three words – viz. yoga (the path of selfless action with devotion), sanyasa (renunciation) and tyaga (sacrifice or relinquishment).

Reader is faced with the doubts mainly due to the conflicting definitions given in Bhagavad Gita to sanyasa and tyaga.

Reader explains his position as follows: **Sanyasi** has been defined as 'one who discharges the duty without attachment to its fruits' – in chapter 6 – 1. It has also been stated therein that sanyasi is also a yogi. It is further clarified that sanyasi is not the one who has abandoned his duties such as lighting sacred fire and performance of rites.

Now, let us turn to the definition of **tyaga** as expounded in chapter 18 – 2. Tyaga is defined as 'the abandonment of the fruits of all duties', which is quite similar to the definition given to sanyasa.

Bhagavad Gita has declared that sanyasa and yoga are one. But there is no such statement to the effect indicating that sanyasa and tyaga are one.

A different definition for sanyasi is also given in chapter 18 – 2 – viz. abandonment of all desire prompted actions.

Reader, troubled with such doubts like Arjuna's dilemma in the battlefield, has moved towards the temple for worship. On his return, he sees his three friends – **Scholar, Devotee and Critic,** discussing the various aspects of Bhagavad Gita in the precinct of the temple in a corner unmindful of the surroundings.

Reader: It is God sent gift that all the three are assembled here, as I can clear my doubts in Bhagavad Gita.

Devotee: O, Reader! It is good that you have faith in us.

Critic: Faith alone cannot clear doubts. Anyhow, we can either clear your doubts or create more doubts!

All laugh.

Scholar: O, Reader! Even doubts can be considered good, provided they are cleared soon. First chapter of Bhagavad Gita is titled as 'yoga of Arjuna's dilemma'. Here even dilemma has become yoga. It is because Arjuna's mind is pure and has taken complete refuge in Sri Bhagavan Krishna for guidance.

Devotee: Yes, for the doubting soul, only ruin awaits, no happiness or salvation, as per Sri Krishna of Bhagavad Gita.

Critic: Let us hear Reader's doubts.

Reader explains his doubts in detail as indicated above.

Scholar: In chapter 18 –2, it has been stated that sanyasi has to abandon all ritualistic actions (kamya karma) motivated by desires with promises of specific rewards leaving routine and ascetic actions untouched. Sri Krishna's final view regarding abandonment of work for sanyasi is that only desire prompted works need be abandoned and that devotional and altruistic works like worship, austerity and gift should be performed by all – including sanyasi because they are holy and sanctifying.

Critic: Tyagi is expected to do all karma – but is to renounce only the fruits of those actions. Sanyasi is asked to abandon only kamya karma. The fate of other karmas – whether they are to be performed renouncing the fruits thereof – is left unanswered.

Scholar: Viewed the issue in a broader perspective, it is advisable to treat yoga, sanyasa and tyaga as one – the distinction only in nomenclature.

Reader: While explaining the concept of sanyasa and yoga in chapter 5 – 1 to 3, Bhagavad Gita suddenly brings into picture – samkhya (knowledge) and yoga in chapter 5 – 4 & 5. Again, in the next immediate stanza - chapter 5 – 6, Bhagavad Gita reverts back to sanyasa.

Critic: It is a real test question. Let me give the contents of the text referred to above.

Bhagavad Gita states that to speak of yoga of knowledge and action as different is only childish and it is not a statement from the wise. A person, who has truly mastered one, gets the benefits of both. The state, which attains by yoga of knowledge, that same state is attained by yoga of action too. He who sees both knowledge and selfless action as one sees truly.

The question of doubt of Reader is this: 'The subject matter discussed in the chapter is action and its abandonment only. Hence, the knowledge factor, which is 'action less', seems to be out of context and distracts the main sequence.'

Scholar: Here again, there are no contradictions.

Action can be physical or mental or both. In yoga of knowledge, there is no physical or body action, but mental action is prevalent. Similarly, yoga of action has both physical and mental actions. Hence in yoga of knowledge, knowledge is accompanied by abandonment of work – thereby achieving the state of Brahman. Hence, we can reasonably conclude that though the paths of knowledge for sanyasa and tyaga are different, the goals are the same to them.

Reader: The word 'tyaga' is used only in chapter 18 in five stanzas and it has not been found in any other chapters. The word sanyasa is used in around 17 stanzas – majority of them found in chapters 5 & 6. But the most extensively used word is yoga in Bhagavad Gita.

Critic: 'Yoga' itself is a big topic for discussion. I think that stanza 12 in chapter 18 needs a close look, which may throw some light on sanyasa and tyaga episode.

Scholar: Well said, O, Critic! The stanza will definitely strengthen my view that sanyasa and tyaga are one.

What that stanza states is this: 'For non-tyagis, the three fold fruit of action – evil, good and mixed – accrue after death. For sanyasi, these will never accrue.' That means 'the benefits or rewards for abandonment of fruits of action do not accrue either to tyagi or sanyasi and attachment to fruits of action is considered a bondage.' By this, tyagi and sanyasi stand in the same position without much difference in them. Hence tyagi and sanyasi can be treated alike to get a clearer picture, which will eschew all unnecessary doubts and dilemma.

Critic: O, Scholar! Really a scholarly answer to the questions posed to us!

I am hastened to add that the mathematical equations, if applied for the statements and definitions pertaining to yoga, sanyasa and tyaga, will give us a better solution to the doubts raised by the Reader. By specific statement, sanyasa = yoga and by definition, sanyasa = tyaga. Hence by derivation, tyaga = yoga. Therefore, by conclusion and comparison of the above equations, yoga = sanyasa = tyaga.

Scholar: O, Critic! Wonderful and the buck of doubts should stop here. Yoga is confined to action and samkhya (knowledge) is reserved for knowledge. This is the concept enumerated in the beginning of Bhagavad Gita, but in the process, yoga encompasses both karma (action) and gnana (knowledge).

Sanskrit word 'yoga' has its root in 'yuga' meaning 'yoke'. Hence 'yoke' is applied to control body, soul, mind, senses, intellect and ego so as to attain peace and bliss as the ultimate goal.

Yoga is a supreme word – having a powerful connotation. It is a common connecting link to give a spiritual content to anything in which it has been associated. Sri Krishna in Bhagavad Gita declares: 'Yogi is superior to ascetic, superior to men of knowledge and superior to ritualists. Therefore, O, Arjuna! Be a Yogi.'

In another instance, Sri Krishna says: 'O, Arjuna, you are born with divine qualities.'

It is worthwhile to recapitulate that Sri Krishna does not want Arjuna to become sanyasi, gnani, tyagi or ritualist but urges him to become a yogi!

Reader: If yoga is superior to sanyasa, then Critic's equations attract amendments. O, Scholar! Please clarify.

Scholar: Critic's mathematical equations are acceptable, but they need amendments. Bhagavad Gita also says that yoga is superior to sanyasa (ch.5 – 1 & 2) and that the relative mathematical equation is yoga > sanyasa. But, yoga = sanyasa as explained - (ch.6 – 1 & 2). Hence, the formulae can be yoga > & = sanyasa depending upon the quality factor of yoga and sanyasa at the material time.

Critic: Sanyasa is normally associated with giving up of worldly pleasures especially practice of brahmacharya (celibacy). But there is no mention about it, when dealing with sanyasa in Bhagavad Gita. The word "Brahmacharya" occurs only once in dealing with the method and practice of meditation. (ch.6 – 14).

Scholar: Yoga is the control of body, mind, senses, intellect and ego that has been vividly explained in Bhagavad Gita. Control of all is important and there is no necessity to give importance to the control of sex organ alone that is the main plank of brahmacharia.

Chapter 5 is titled as 'yoga of sanyasa' and hence what has been stated therein can be taken as a final word in so far as sanyasa is concerned.

To sum up, Bhagavad Gita reiterates in the chapter as under: Though sanyasa and karma both lead to freedom, karma is superior to sanyasa. Sanyasi does not hate or desire and he is free from the pair of opposites like heat and cold, pleasure and pain, victory and defeat, gain and loss. Sanyasa and karma are the same, as the fruits obtained from the both are the same.

Critic: Mere title of the chapter cannot be construed to give finality to the topic of sanyasa. More than the concept of sanyasa, the topic dealt in that chapter is more on 'yoga' than 'sanyasa'. The references to sanyasa are restricted to 3 stanzas while yoga is referred to in 8 stanzas.

Scholar: This will only buttress my statement that sanyasa is also yoga. Here it is worthwhile to note the statement in Bhagavad Gita declaring that tyaga is satvika in nature (ch.18 – 9). Sanyasa is also satvika in nature, as satvika nature – pure and luminous – binds soul to the body with joy and wisdom and it moves soul upwards and is the most beneficial to soul to reach heaven.

In the same way, sanyasin, on shedding his lust and anger and subduing his mind, is said to attain the beatitude of Brahman both here and hereafter (ch.5 – 26).

Critic: Here again, there is no direct statement to equate sanyasa with satvika as in the case of tyaga. Anyhow, your scholarly derivations and interpretations are non-disputable and have to be accepted.

Devotee: I like to remind you all Sri Krishna's famous declarations in Bhagavad Gita which runs like this: 'You abode in this teaching of Mine, full of faith and free from trivial objections. Those who find fault at My teachings and act not thereon, deluded in all knowledge and devoid of discrimination, know them to be ruined.'

Critic: O, Devotee! Have you forgotten the immortal teachings of Sri Krishna who has this to say: 'Approach the seers with all respects and humiliation and service and they will clear you of your doubts and show the path of knowledge?'

Reader: Let me conclude taking the cue from Arjuna. 'O, My Friends! My doubts are cleared. I have regained my wisdom through your deliberations. Now, I am at peace.'

Article 9 - My Dilemma on superiority of Karma over Sanyasa

Kindly refer to the above article 8 wherein Karma yoga and Sanyasa yoga are discussed. It is stated in the article that Karma yoga is superior to Sanyasa yoga because Sanyasa yoga is difficult to perform, though both has the same objective or goal. (Refer: ch.5 – 2 - Superior & 6 - Difficult)

Bhagavad Gita's sloka 6 of chapter 5 states: It is not easy to become a Karma Sanyasi without Karma yoga. Muni – meaning Karma Sanyasi through performance of Karma yoga soon reaches brahman.

Actually, Krishna before asserting 'Karma yoga is superior to Sanyasa yoga', He says: Both yogas lead to the same goal of souls' liberations. Hence as both yogas' goals are the same, both yogas become equal in status none being superior to the other. Superiority tag cannot be given on this basis.

The reasoning given in the sloka for giving a superior tag to Karma is this: Karma yoga is a must for one who wants to become Karma sanyasi. Rather it can be assumed that one attains the position of Sanyasa yoga only after his successful performance as Karma yogi. This indicates that Karma yoga's tag vanishes, when one becomes succeeded in reaching his status of Sanyasa.

Superiority cannot be decided on the basis of easy and difficult task to be accomplished. In fact, if the task is difficult, it can be tagged as superior and vice versa.

But here it is reverse.

Then can we conclude Krishna is wrong?

No – Never.

Let us analyse.

The maya of dilemma between Karma and Sanyasa yogas is purely due to clinging to the bare words and phrases devoid of their deep philosophical and spiritual meanings embedded in them.

Bhagavad Gita – chapter 5 titled as Sanyasa yogam with 29 slokas if analysed carefully, one can understand that Karma yoga forms the foundation for Sanyasa yoga thereby its importance being emphasised.

Nomenclatures of sannyasa (used in ch.5- slokas 1 and 3), both sanyasa and karma yoga (used in ch.5 – sloka 2), sakhyam/karma sanyasam and yoga (used in ch.5 – slokas 4 & 5) and yogi (used in slokas 11 & 24) are worth to make note of.

Mostly the aspects of Karma yoga and Karma Sannyasa are explained in detail therein. These slokas will remove the veil of confusion and dilemma in toto from one's mind pertaining to tag of superiority attached to Karma yoga as compared to Sanyasa yoga.

Further, though entire chapter is for Sanyasa yoga, Krishna narrates the experiences, characteristics and qualities of Karma yogis which will buttress the superiority of karma yogis over sanyasis.

It is revealed in Bhagavad Gita that Karma sanyasa is difficult to attain without Karma yoga and that Karma yogi attains supreme quickly compared to Sanyasa yoga. This will tag Karma yoga as superior than Sanyasa yoga.

First, human being - embodied soul has to be trained under the able guidance of Karma yogi to become Sanyasa yogi. Literally human being becomes a disciple of Karma yogi to get fully trained in the realms of Karma yoga – performing actions without attachments i.e., relinquishing the fruits of actions. After human being's training under Karma yogi is over, it becomes eligible to practice Sanyasa yoga. By this aspect, Karma yogi becomes Guru to Sanyasa yogi. Because of this alone, Krishna puts superiority tag to Karma yoga.

Base for Sanyasa is Karma yoga with which Sanyasi raises his temple of spiritual secluded ascetic life and becomes friend, philosopher and guide to the society at large.

Life of Sanyasi is very difficult, as he has to live a simple life keeping his needs to barest minimum. Foremost, he has to guard his celibacy at all times. If he fails, then it will be fatal and he will be doomed for ever. Even his past good deeds will not come to his rescue, as it is a complete loss for him. But, in respect of Karma yoga, human being practicing Karma yoga, even if he fails, he will have the benefits of his past good karma that will give him an advantage to be born in a religious and spiritual house. His past good deeds will put him in the position of his past birth from where he failed.

Hence Karma yoga is superior than Sanyasa yoga however much Sanyasa yoga is difficult to follow for human beings.

Article 10 - Yoga

Preface: The purpose of this article is to bring out the tenets of yoga as explained by Sri Krishna in Bhagavad Gita. There are eighteen chapters in Bhagavad Gita and at the end of every chapter, title of the chapter is narrated as under: 'Thus, in the Upanishad of the Bhagavad Gita containing the dialogue between Sri Krishna and Arjuna … ends with chapter title as 'yoga of ……(name of the subject being mentioned)'. By this, one can very much understand that yoga is the main link of the entire message of Sri Krishna. Sri Krishna is praised as the Lord of Yoga in Bhagavad Gita.

The words – yoga, yogam and yogins – are mentioned on the whole in Bhagavad Gita in 76 stanzas of which maximum number of 29 stanzas is confined to chapter 6 – Yoga of Meditation. This goes to show that yoga and meditation or to be precise – yoga and mind have a direct bearing between them. Hence, it is to be understood that yoga is mainly to control mind.

Reader, Scholar, Devotee and Critic have assembled to discuss 'Yoga'.

Reader: Bhagavad Gita says about yoga thus:

Yoga means yoga of action with devotion.

Yoga of action with devotion means selfless action.

Selfless action means action without attachment to the fruits of action.

Selfless action is possible only with the evenness of mind.

Evenness of mind means evenness in success and failure, virtue and vice and it is possible only by control of sense organs by control of mind.

Control of mind is possible by practice of meditation.

Scholar: To concise what Reader has said, is this: Yoga means Purity, Perfection and Peace of mind pertaining to knowledge, action and devotion.

Devotee: Yoga is immortal, ancient and supreme secret. Yoga was first imparted by Sri Krishna to Sun God and Yoga is to be known from the teacher as a disciple. Yoga is to be imparted only to a friend and devotee.

Scholar: Karma is said to be the means of the sage who seeks to attain to yoga. Once he attained yoga, mind becomes calm. With this state of mind, one will treat alike a lump of earth, a stone, a piece of gold and he is said to attain the steadfastness in spiritual communication. Hence, he is fit to attain Brahman.

Critic: In disturbed water, the image will not be visible. Similarly, God will not be seen, when the mind is disturbed by the desires and lust.

Reader: Yoga is the destroyer of pain – whether it is body or mind. Yogi is also sinless. Yogi is regarded as the best, when he treats pleasure and pain as the same on account of the perception of the same Atman in all. Yoga is to treat all with impartiality.

Devotee: Rusted iron will not be attracted by magnet. Similarly, if the mind is deluded with the likes and dislikes like rust, there will arise no devotion to God.

Scholar: The nature of the mind can be understood clearly with the following factor. Milk in the vessel will boil till the fire below is burning. Once the fire is put out, the boiling stops. Similarly, mind of the yogi will be boiling with equanimity till the fire of yoga practices persists.

Critic: To attain the status of Best Yogi, is not that easy due to Yoga Maya. All beings are subject to illusion even from their births due to likes and dislikes born out of desires. Further Sri Krishna is veiled in Yoga-Maya (Divine Power) and hence Sri Krishna is not revealed to all. Thus, this deluded world does not know Sri Krishna – the unborn and unchanging.

Reader: Devotion to Sri Krishna is the simplest form of Yoga, which can be practised by all.

Scholar: The following narrations will enlighten the status of three stages of persons.

There are three dolls made up of salt, cloth and stone each. When the three dolls are immersed in water, the salt doll loses its form and melts with water. The cloth doll swallows water and the third stone doll is not affected by water.

The first salt doll realises the supreme and reaches Him. The second is affected by the water and is like a devotee to the Supreme. The stone doll is completely ignorant of the Supreme due to worldly desires.

Devotee: Yoga is also to know the glory and power of God. Best Yoga of worship is worship of manifested God. To know Sri Krishna, practise Yoga.

Scholar: In the darkness, light focused on others reveals them, but not the holder of the light, unless the light is turned towards the holder. Similarly, God sees all but human beings to get His attention should follow the paths of Yogas. Then God will turn his torch towards Himself and such devotees become blessed souls.

That is the purpose of Yoga for human souls.

Article 11 - Meditation

Sri Krishna is called Lord of Meditation. It is because Sri Krishna explains meditation in Bhagavad Gita.

Specific stanzas about modalities of meditation can be found in about 13 places – viz. ch.2 – stanza 66, ch. 4 – stanza 29, ch.5 – stanzas 27 & 28, ch.6 – stanzas 10 to 18.

Sri Krishna has devoted to meditation entire chapter 6 appropriately titled as Yoga of Meditation. Let us know about meditation from the mouth of Sri Krishna Himself.

What are the prerequisites for meditation?

Sri Krishna speaks: One who eats too much, or who does not eat at all and who sleeps too much or too little, is not fit for meditation. One who is moderate in eating, recreation, working, sleeping and walking, is fit for meditation.

What are the preparations for meditation?

Sri Krishna speaks: On selecting a pure and secluded place, a seat of three layers – need to be made – bottom layer being kusha grass, middle one a black antelope skin and the uppermost being a cloth. This seat should be laid on a place which is neither very much raised nor very low.

What is the posture of the body while on meditation?

Sri Krishna speaks: One should hold body, head and neck erect, motionless and firm. One should concentrate on tip of the nose without any distractions.

How does one practice meditation?

Sri Krishna speaks: One who practices meditation is required to fix his look between the eyebrows. He should steady flow of the breaths in a rhythmic way – during inhalation and exhalation through nostrils, one who meditates, has to control mind and intellect from onslaughts of desires, fear and anger.

Why does one practice meditation?

Sri Krishna speaks:

"Meditation can control mind which gets purified and the resultant factor is peace of mind. Project entire self towards ME and the summit of bliss is within reach. And such a meditation will lead the self to MY ABODE. As the flame of a lamp sheltered from wind does not flicker, the one who meditates as per My dictates, will be united with ME."

Chapter 12 - Corporate Yoga

Be alone.

Seek a solitary spot.

Selected spot should be clean.

Selected spot should neither be too high nor too low.

Spread a cloth on the floor.

Firmly seated on it, practise Breathing Exercise or

Pranayama.

Steps for Breathing Exercise or Pranayama:

1. First Stage:

Breathe with both noses in a measured way, in and out for some time. Practise this for a few days.

2. Second Stage:

Slowly fill the lungs with breath through the left nostril and then hold the breath for some time. For beginners, holding of the breath is for four seconds and slowly it can be increased. Release the breath slowly through the right nostril.

Repeat the breathing in the same with the right nostril.

This is one Pranayama.

3. Third Stage:

Draw the breath with the both noses in and then throw the breath immediately out slowly – without holding it as above. This is easier one.

Note:

Pranayama is divided into three parts:

Filling, Restraining, and Emptying.

Lowest Pranayama: 12 seconds.

Middle Pranayama: 24 seconds.

Best Pranayama: 36 seconds.

Article 13 – Practicing Meditation by Swami Vivekannda

Preface:

In Bhagavad Gita, Sri Bhagavan Krishna gives importance to Meditation, as the mind is the most difficult organ to control. 'Mind is Monkey' phrase is enough to indicate how much difficult it will be to keep mind under control.

Meditation is the best method to control the mind.

Swami Vivekananda had written in detail how one can control the monkey mind through the practice of meditation. I thought that it will be ideal if the passages are reproduced for the benefit of the readers.

These pages are from chapter 5 – The Control of Psychic Prana – pages 166 to 170 & chapter 8 – Raja Yoga in Brief - page 191 from the complete works of Swami Vivekananda – Volume 1 – Published by Advaita Ashrama, Calcutta.

- Author.

1. **The Control of Psychic Prana**

Pranayama is to control the motion of the lungs. Mind has become externalized and hence lost sight of finer motions of lungs inside. One needs to feel the lung's motions to control them. Continuous exercises of Pranayama help to control motion of lungs.

Exercise of Pranayama:

First part: Sit upright. Body must be kept straight. The three parts of the body – the chest, the neck and the head – must be always held straight in one line.

Second part: Control nerves. Nerve centre that controls the respiratory organs has a controlling effect on the other nerves. Hence to control nerves, rhythmic breathing is necessary.

The breathing that we generally use should not be called breathing at all. Hence Pranayama helps to have rhythmic breathing.

First Lesson in rhythmic breathing is just to breathe in a measured way – in and out. That will harmonise the system. While doing this breathing exercise, chant some sacred words such as "OM".

Let sacred word OM flow in and out with the breath, rhythmically, harmoniously, and you will find the whole body is becoming rhythmical. This exercise will be a real rest – sleep is not a real rest. Once this real rest comes, the most tired nerves will be calmed down, and you will find that you have never before really rested.

After practicing the above-mentioned breathing exercise for a few days, you should take up a higher one.

Here it is:

Slowly fill the lungs with breath through the Ida, the left nostril, and at the same time concentrate the mind on the nerve current.

You are, as it were, sending the nerve current down the spinal column, and striking violently on the last plexus, the basic lotus which is triangular in form, the seat of the Kundalini. Then hold the current there for some time.

Imagine that you are slowly drawing that nerve current with the breath through the other side, the Pingala, then slowly throw it out through the right nostril. This you will find a little difficult to practice. The easiest way is to stop the right nostril with the thumb, and then slowly draw in the breath through the left; then close both nostrils with thumb and forefinger, and imagine that you are sending that current down, and striking the base of the Subhuman; then take the thumb off, and let the breath out through the right nostril.

Next inhale slowly through the right nostril, keeping the other closed by the forefinger, then close both as before.

Lungs should be prepared for this exercise and hence it is well to begin with four seconds, and slowly increase. Draw in four seconds, hold in sixteen seconds, then throw out in eight seconds. This makes one Pranayama.

At the same time think of the basic lotus, triangular in form; concentrate the mind on that centre. The imagination can help you a great deal.

The next breathing is slowly drawing the breath in, and then immediately throwing it out slowly, and then stopping the breath out, using the same numbers. The only difference is that in the first case the breath was held in, and in the second held out.

The last is the easiest one. The breathing in which you hold the breath in the lungs must not be practiced too much. Do it only four times in the morning, and four times in the evening. Then you can slowly increase the time and number.

Of the three processes for the purification of the nerves, described above, the first and the last are neither difficult nor dangerous. The more you practice the first one the calmer you will be. Just think of "OM" and you can practice even when you are sitting at your work.

The Yogis claim that of all the energies that are in the human body the highest is what they call "OJAS". Now this Ojas is in a man's hand, the more powerful he is, the more intellectual, the more spiritually strong. One man may speak beautiful language and beautiful thoughts, but they do not impress people; another man speaks neither beautiful language nor beautiful thoughts, yet his words charm. Every movement of his is powerful. That is the power of OJAS.

All the forces that are working in the body in their highest become OJAS.

The Yogis say that that part of the human energy which is expressed as sex energy, in sexual thought, when checked into OJAS and as the Muladhara guides these, the Yogis pays particular attention to that centre. He tries to take up all his sexual energy and convert it into OJAS. It is only the chase man or woman who can make the OJAS rise and store it in the brain; that is why chastity has always been considered the highest virtue.

There must be perfect chastity in thought, word, and deed; without it the practice of Raja-Yoga is dangerous, and may lead to insanity.

2. Raja Yoga in brief

Pranayama consists of Prana and Ayama. Prana means the vital forces in one's own body, Ayama means controlling them.

There are three sorts of Pranayama, the very simple, the middle and the very high.

Pranayama is divided into three parts:

1. Filling; 2. Restraining; 3. Emptying.

When you begin with 12 seconds, it is the lowest Pranayama; when you begin with 24 seconds, it is the middle Pranayama; that Pranayama is the best which begins with 36 seconds.

In the lowest kind of Pranayama there is perspiration, in the medium kind, quivering of the body and in the highest Pranayama levitation of the body and influx of great bliss.

There is a Mantra called the Gayatri. It is very holy verse of the Vedas.

'We meditate on the glory of that Being who has produced this universe; May He enlighten our minds;"

OM is joined to it at the beginning and the end.

In one Pranayama repeat three Gayathris.

In all books they speak of Pranayama being divided into Rechaka (rejecting or exhaling), Puraka (inhaling), and Kumbhaka (restraining, stationary).

The Indriyas, the organs of the senses, are acting outwards and coming in contact with external objects. Bringing them under the control of the will is what is called Pratyahara or gathering towards oneself.

Fixing the mind on the lotus of the heart, or on the centre of the head, is what is called Dharana.

Limited to one spot, making that spot the base, a particular kind of mental waves rises; these are not swallowed up by other kinds of waves, but by degrees become prominent, while all the others recede and finally disappear.

Next the multiplicity of these waves gives place to unity and one wave only is left in the mind. This is Dhyana meditation. When no basis is necessary, when the whole of the mind has become one wave, one-formedness, it is called Samadhi.

Bereft of all help from places and centres, only the meaning of the thought is present. If the mind can be fixed on the centre for 12 seconds, it will be a Dharana, 12 such Dharanas will be a Dhyana, and 12 such Dhyanas will be a Samadhi.

Dhyana is spoken of, and a few examples are given of what to meditate upon.

Sit straight, and look at the tip of your nose. Later on, we shall come to know how that concentrates the mind, how by controlling the two optic nerves one advances a long way towards the control of the arc of reaction, and so to the control of the will.

Here are a few specimens of meditation.

Imagine a lotus upon the top of the head, several inches up, with virtue as its centre, and knowledge as its stalk. The eight petals of the lotus are the eight powers of the Yogi.

Inside, the stamens and pistils are renunciation.

If the Yogi refuses the external powers he will come to salvation. So, the eight petals of the lotus are the eight powers, but the internal stamens and pistils are extreme renunciation, the renunciation of all these powers. Inside of that lotus think of the Golden One, the Almighty, the Intangible. He whose name is OM, the Inexpressible, surrounded with effulgent light, Meditate on that.

Another meditation is given. Think of a space in your heart, and in the midst of that space think that a flame is burning. Think of that flame as your own soul and inside the flame is another effulgent light, and that is the Soul of your soul, God.

Meditate upon that in the heart.

OM Shanthi OM Shanthi OM Shanthi.

Article 14 - Prana and Apana

Bhagavad Gita of chapter 4 – 29 and chapter 15 – 14 deals with Prana and Apana.

Gnana and Sanyasa Yoga (Yoga of Knowledge and Renunciation) of chapter 4 and Purushothama Yoga (Yoga of Supreme Self) of chapter 15 mention about the most important subtle air energy which is a vital force for meditation.

Bhagavad Gita of chapter 4 – 29 mentions Prana and Apana as under: Practice of Pranayama is of regulating vital air energies of Prana and Apana. Consign Prana in Apana and Apana in Prana in sacrificial fire.

Bhagavad Gita of chapter 15 – sloka 14 mentions Prana and Apana as under: Vaishvanara – Fire of Digestion resides inside the body. Vital subtle air energies called Prana and Apana digest four types of food taken by human. (Note: Four types of food are solid, liquid, semi solid and semi liquid foods. When taken, digestive fire residing in the belly burns solid food after biting, liquid food after drinking, semi-solid food after chewing and semi liquid food after licking.)

Brief explanations of Prana and Apana:

Prana means energy and yama means control. Hence Pranayama practice means to control breaths to calm senses and mind. This holding of breath builds energy within body.

There are five types of vayus or breaths as follows:

1. Prana vayu (inward moving breath): Responsible for our eating of food

2. Apana vayu (downward moving breath): Responsible to eliminate waste material,

3. Samana vayu (equalising breath): Digests food.

4. Udana vayu (ascending breath): Circulates nutrients around the body,

5. Vyanu vayu (diffusive breath): To utilise the energy derived for physical activity.

Each Vayu controls a specific area of body and ideally functions in harmony with each other. Vayus affect and influence our physical, emotional and mental health and wellness. If a Vayu becomes imbalanced, body is affected.

Prana Vayu: Prana-Vayu is situated in heart, and its energy pervades chest region. This Vayu is fundamental energy in body and directs and feeds into four other Vayus. When prana vayu is weak, mind cannot focus and experiences excess worry.

Apana-Vayu: Apana-Vayu is situated in pelvic region and its energy pervades lower abdomen. Organs of digestion, reproduction, and elimination are influenced by this vayu.

Samana vayu: Samana means balance and it is a balancing breath – middle breath. Samana is essential energy of digestion, and as such brings vitality to digestive system and its associated organs.

Vyana-Vayu: Vyana-Vayu is situated in heart and lungs and flows throughout entire body. Its function is to circulate all substances throughout body and rendering assistants to other vayus for their proper functions.

Udana-Vayu: Udana-Vayu is situated in throat and it has a circular flow around neck and head. It governs speech and self-expression.

There is a saying - 'Annam Prana Mayam' – Cooked Rice (or Food in general) is All Prana. This statement is enough to emphasise the importance of both Prana amongst other vayus and rice amongst other food articles.

Prana Vayu is main vayu and other four vayus are its tributaries. Prana Vayu is life energy and its symbol is OM.

Article 15 - Sri Krishna as Lord of Action

Sri Krishna said that there was nothing in all three worlds for Him to do, yet He continued to work because Sri Krishna is Lord of Action.

(Main References: Ch.3, stanzas 9, 16, 17, 18, 19, 22, 23, 24 - Refer page no. 30)

Critical Comments:

Sacrificial duty keeps the wheel of creation in motion. Those who rejoice in sense pleasure with no sacrificial duties are said to lead vain and sinful lives.

A mirror, which is full of dust, cannot reflect any image. When you remove the dust with a piece of cloth, your image is clearly visible. Mirror is like your mind and dust is Ego born out of lust, greed and anger. The piece of cloth, which removes the dust, is selfless service to the humanity which includes sacrificial duties.

Mind becomes pure on performance of selfless service. For them, Work is worship.

A few men abandoning the world seek the silence of the forest land where they do penance to achieve enlightenment and salvation. Such sages perform no action and they also do not depend upon others for anything – their needs are minimal and self-sufficient.

Sun light, when it passes through a lens, converges into a bright spot, which is capable of burning cotton. Heat energy, which is inherent in the sunlight, is focused. But, when the same sun light, when it is allowed to pass through a prism, splits into many radiant and colourful rays spreading its wings of light wide enough to cover the entire room. The sage, who is seeking salvation for him, is akin to the lens and the man who is involved in services to the mankind, is compared to the prism. Heat energy of the lens is penance and colourful rays of the prism are selfless service.

Wheel of the Universe is to be kept at motion always so that the activities of birth, evolution and death are kept alive. Sri Krishna is omnipresent, omniscient and omnipotent and hence there is nothing for Him to perform. Yet, as role model for the humans, He performs, as otherwise humans also will become idle beings. Sri Krishna is King of Actions.

Article 16 – Sanyasam is Yogam

Selfless action is means to attain heights of yoga. Hence, renouncement of selfish motive of an action which is the characteristic of sanyasi is yoga.

(Main Reference: Ch.5 – stanza 13, Ch.6 – stanza 1,2,3,4) – Refer page no. 31)

Critical Comments:

Yogi and sanyasi achieve purity of Mind. Purity of Mind leads to peace of Mind.

How does one achieve Purity of Mind?

Mind is also a sense organ like eyes, ears, nose, mouth, and skin. But mind is not a tangible object like other organs. Activity of mind is thinking. Suppliers for mind's activities are other sense organs through sight, sound, smell, speech and touch. Thoughts of mind may be bad, good or pure. Capacity to hold thoughts by mind depends upon its memory. Memory is controlled by Time. Time erases Memory due to power of Forgetfulness.

Intellect getting support from Consciousness is the gatekeeper of mind. Intellect filters thoughts and helps to prevent bad ones to enter mind. But all cannot afford to have the gatekeeper and hence mind is filled with all bad thoughts in many human beings.

Vehicles of Bad thoughts are Desires driven by Lust, Anger and Greed. Such Bad thoughts gate-crash into Mind defeating Gatekeeper Intellect and mind is filled with bad thoughts. Mind is unable to withstand the pressure and hence it bursts leading to havoc in one's life. Sense organs become ferocious and uncontrollable. Man becomes murderer, robber or commits suicide. Hence control of mind means control of bad thoughts, which in turn means controls over lust, anger and greed.

Water is bad, good or pure depending upon its quality. To remove badness (impurities) from water, water is to be boiled. Water becomes good on boiling. To make water pure, it should be boiled further till water becomes steam. Fire is required to make water good and pure. Similarly, when Mind is heated, bad thoughts will be destroyed leaving behind good thoughts and further heating process will make mind pure.

Fire to heat the mind comes from Meditation, Prayer, Pilgrimage and Recitation/Listening of Scriptures. Intensity of Meditation and other means is the measure of mind's purity. Constant practice and vigil are necessary to have the purity of mind at all times.

Let there be Purity of Mind, which leads to Peace of Mind.

Article 17 - Fruits of Action

Normally motive for action is its fruits. To elevate action to Karma level, action should be performed without minding rewards which is called non-attachment to the fruits of action. At the same time, non-attachment to the fruits of action should not lead into inaction.

(Main reference: Ch. 2 – 47 – Refer page 32)

Critical Comments:

Currency note has no value as a paper, as the paper cannot boil even a cup of water. But the same currency note can buy us enough firewood to boil not only water but also to cook our food. Such is the power of the paper in view of the stamp of authority and approval printed on it. Action becomes powerful, if the action is stamped with 'yoga of action'. Yoga of action here means selfless action or simply action without attachment to the fruits of action.

The phrase – 'Action without attachment to fruits of action' contains two factors – Action or Karma and Non-attachment to fruits of action. The emphasis in the phrase is on 'non-attachment' and not on 'action'. Action is compulsory to all, but performing action without attachment is more important to achieve the purpose of life – salvation. At any stage, man should not be idle – leading a life of inaction.

Performing action without attachment to the fruits does not mean performing action in any way – well or badly. One must not do action badly and then say, "I did not care about the fruits."

Action may be bad or good. Action may be under compulsion, under contract of salary, under obligation. At the lowest level of the animal and the slave, work is the result of force of compulsion. At the higher level of a free man, it springs from profit motive – profit here or in other spheres in the hereafter.

When man grows out of his self-centred outlook, he gets a still higher motivation in occupations involving work for the community, country or humanity. Some others will find a satisfactory scheme of work only when work is dedicated to God. Bhagavad Gita hails the devotion-oriented work without desire for fruits as the best of actions.

A painter devotes his full attention in painting a picture. His outlook is 'art for art's sake.' His aim is only to complete the picture without minding time, his labour or any other factor. When completed, the picture becomes a masterpiece, which may fetch him fame and good price. Though the painter has not aimed for fame or money, the price of dedicated action are really many folds. Similarly, the outlook of a yogi towards action is to treat action as 'act for act's sake'.

The method adopted to catch monkeys will prove how action with attachment ends up in unhappiness. A handful of nuts are put into a jar with a small opening. The monkey puts his hand into the jar, grabs the nuts, and then finds that he cannot get his fist out through the opening. If the monkey would just let go of the nuts, he could escape. But he won't. He is thus caught. Nuts being the object of attachment, which the monkey is holding them tight, becomes the object of unhappiness. Attachment leads to suffering, while Detachment leads to freedom. Freedom leads to happiness.

Article 18 - Eureka Moment for Embodied Soul

Eureka Moment for Embodied Human Soul is the ultimate goal as ordained by Sri Krishna. Eureka Moment is moment of great liberation for human soul to merge with Purushothama who is seated at the top of the roots of Asvattha tree – a strange, holy and world tree having its branches down below to the earth and roots to the sky.

Purushothama seated at the top of roots of Asvattha tree is the witness to the activities of all beings struggling from perennial cycle of births and deaths with a few exceptions of human souls reaching the lotus feet of Almighty Sri Krishna.

Asvattha is Pipal tree that is called 'Arasa Maram' in Tamil which means King Tree. Word asvattha means – highly temporary – not even lasting for tomorrow. Hence it is believed that asvattha tree will be destroyed ultimately at the end of a yuga.

Asvattha tree is strong, long living, holy, auspicious tree. Kings used to tie their horses to that tree and it is believed that it would fetch them victory in the battle. Upper piece of wood of asvattha is used to create fire for yajna by constant churning. Sri Krishna declares that among all the trees I am the Asvattha. It represents the holy symbol of OM, which in turn is the true symbol of the Purushothama.

Asvattha tree is mentioned in Katha Upanishad: "This is the eternal Asvattha tree with its root above and branches below. That root indeed, is called Bright. That is Brahman, and that alone is the immortal. In that, all worlds are contained and none can pass beyond. Most people are used to seeing trees that grow from the ground up, but yogis talk about a tree that grows upside down."

Three Gunas represent branches of asvattha tree, its buds sense objects, its leaves vedas and its roots actions. Detachment is Axe which is a forceful weapon to cut branches of asvattha tree nourished by Gunas.

Allegorical contents of asvattha tree need to be deciphered to understand how the embodied human soul or jivatma struggles to reach heavenly abode of Purushothama to avoid rebirth.

Asvattha tree is like a battle field where jivatma is struggling to reach

Paramatma at the top of the tree. Sense objects of Individual human soul become soldiers who could not be won because individual soul loses its fighting spirit due to deluded mind, intellect and ego. Many individual souls are not in a position to acquire axes of detachment to cut the branches of gunas along with buds. Such souls become equally deaf to the chanting of Vedic lyrics by asvattha' s leaves. Jivatma, due to these failings, is not able to overcome the agony of births and deaths.

Adi Sankara in his Bhajagovndindam song of "Punarabi jananam punarabi maranam" explains this aspect of soul's life clearly and effectively.

Adi Sankara's song means: "Born again, death again, birth again to stay in the mother's womb! It is indeed hard to cross this boundless ocean of samsara. Oh Murari! Redeem me through Thy mercy."

In this allegorical story of Asvattha, Detachment is portrayed as Axe to cut Branch – Gunas and Buds – Sense Objects. Therefore, Axe becomes the main instrument to attain Moksha.

One can reasonably brood over on the making of axe of detachment and such an imaginary interpretation may throw lights to understand the intricacy and implication of spiritual Asvattha tree.

Ironsmith makes axe with heating iron and then hitting it using hammer on anvil that is an important tool in axe manufacture. Guna and sense objects are iron which is heated in a furnace with fuel. Fuel is mind and hammer is intellect. The ego serves as anvil.

Many human souls fail in its attempts to gain access to axes of detachment due to its innate qualities. Actually, axes are not manufactured outside and supplied to human souls. Human soul itself should produce its own axe and then cut the branches of Asvattha happily listening to lyrics of Vedas to reach the roots of Asvattha –

Birthless State.

Tree's Roots are already detached from Earth – foremost element of nature and Sri Krishna sitting on the top of the roots to oversee those human souls to win over other forces of nature – air, fire, water, space to reach his abode. It is the desire and will of Sri Krishna that all embodied human soul or jivatma should use axe to cut branches thereby destroying the World Tree completely at the end of a yuga.

Sri Krishna Avatar ended at the shades of Asvattha tree. On his successful accomplishment of Krishna Avatar, Sri Krishna merged with Purushothama sitting pretty at the top of Asvattha tree. It is the transformation of form to formless almighty.

Eureka Moment while reading the book happening is Sri Bhagavan Krishna's Wish and Blessing.

HARE KRISHNA HARE KRISHNA

KRISHNA KRISHNA HARE HARE

ABOUT THE AUTHOR

❖ Born at Tiruchendur, had schooling there and then graduated at Vivekananda College, Mylapore, Chennai. Employed in State Bank of India – LHO, Chennai as a clerk-typist and then promoted to Officer Cadre and retired at my age of 60.

❖ Influenced by literary, philosophical and religious bent of mind from my young age of 21 years. A few of my Tamil writings mainly short stories - regular and allegorical - were published in some Tamil Monthly Magazines apart from my free style Tamil poems.

❖ Two Free On-Line Monthly Magazines with very limited memberships – E-Touch – English Magazine published for the past 20+ years and Vaaimai – Tamil Monthly Magazine published for the past 16+ years - Both without a break till date – are my unique achievements as an Editor.

❖ Love of Lord Krishna and of His Gospel Bhagavad Gita have resulted in the publication of this book.

www.ingramcontent.com/pod-product-compliance
Lightning Source LLC
LaVergne TN
LVHW031426170726
843492LV00009B/2871

* 9 7 8 8 1 9 6 9 4 2 5 0 2 *